LEGO®

BATMAN THE MOVIE

DC SUPER HEROES UNITE

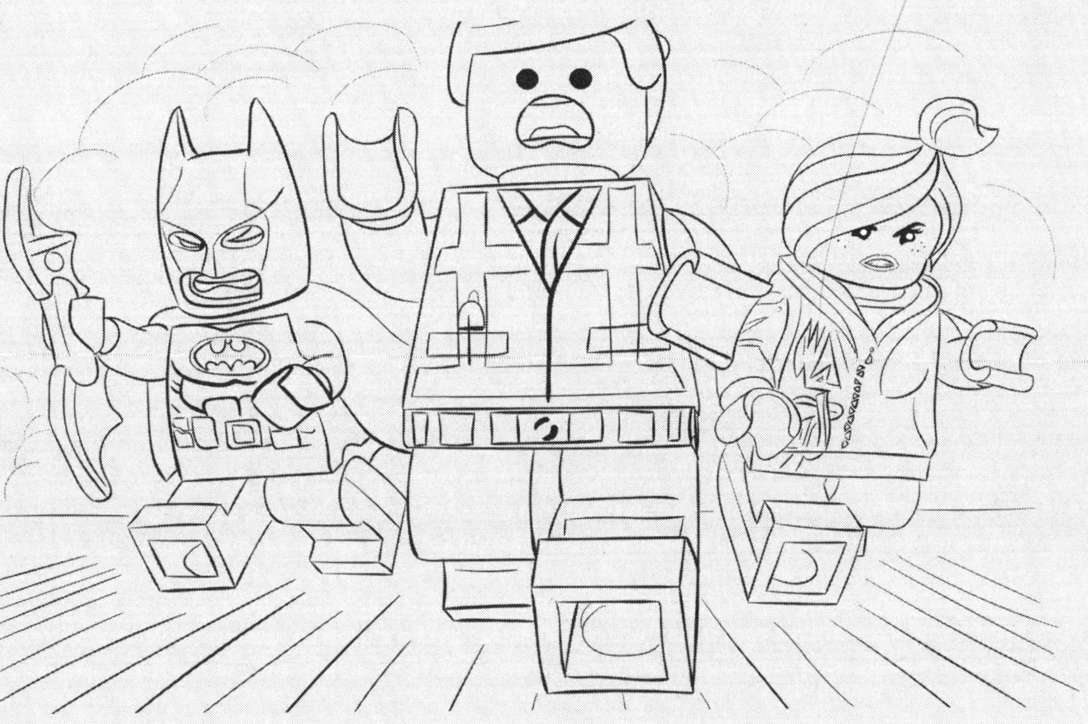

COLORING BOOK

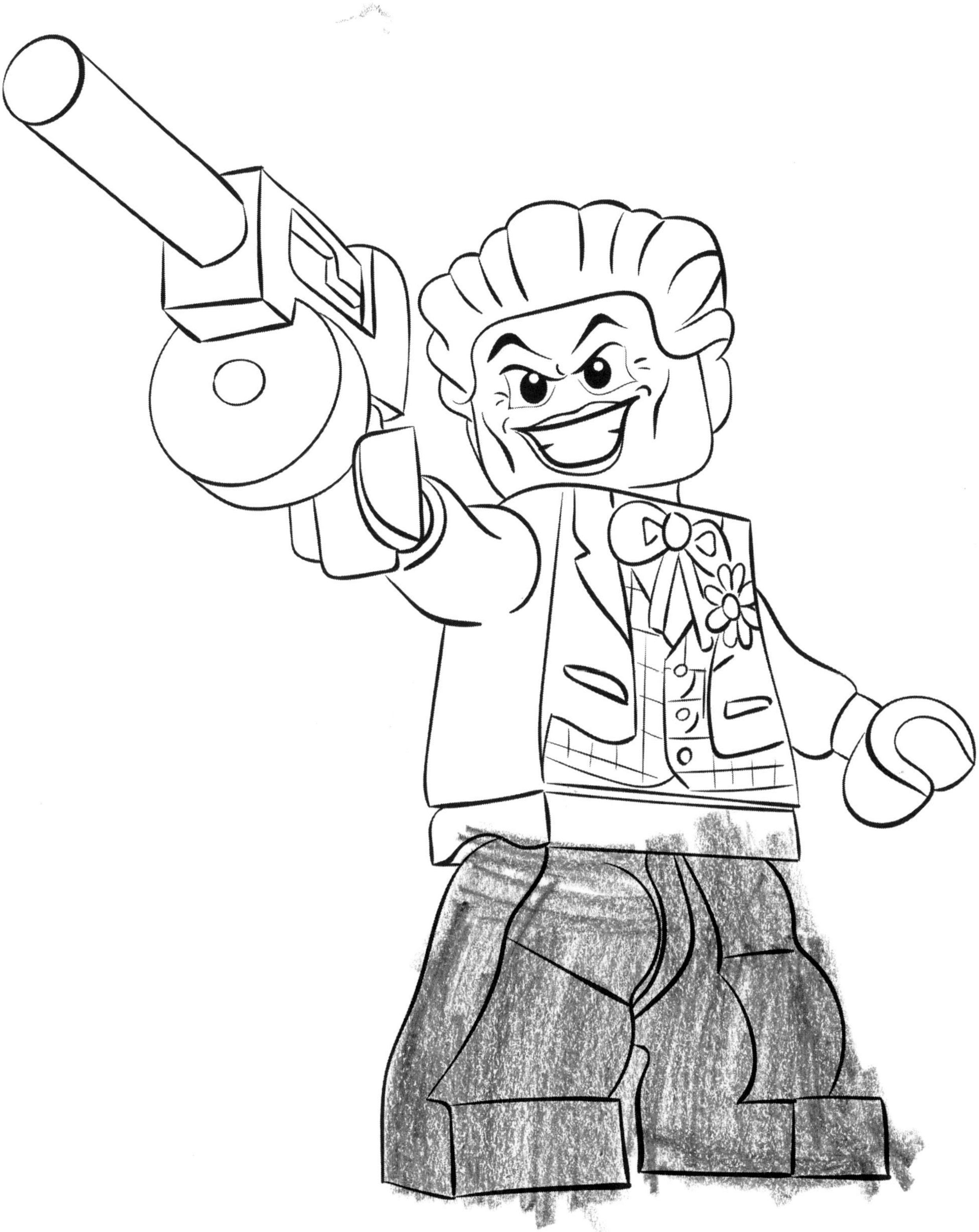

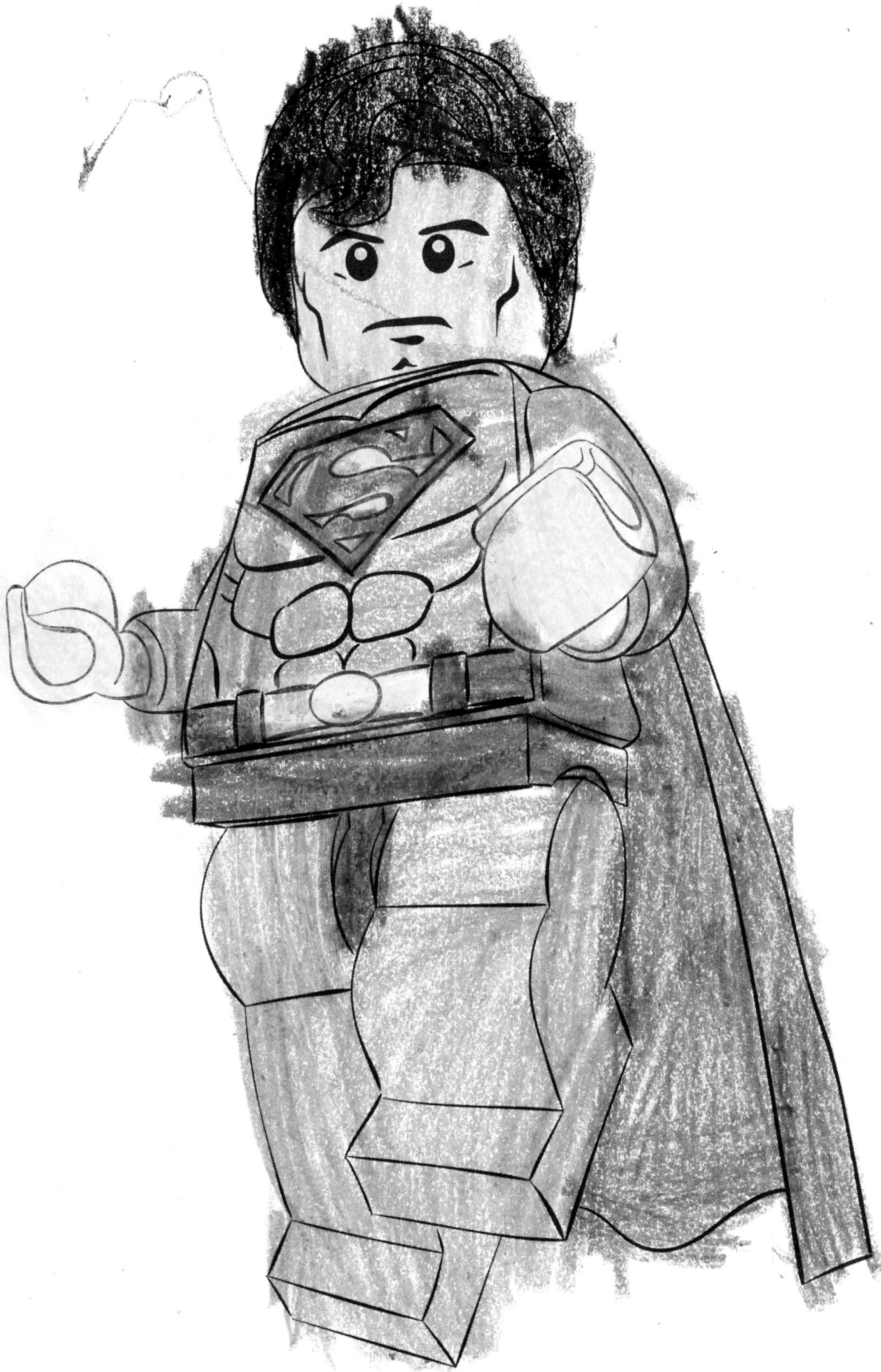

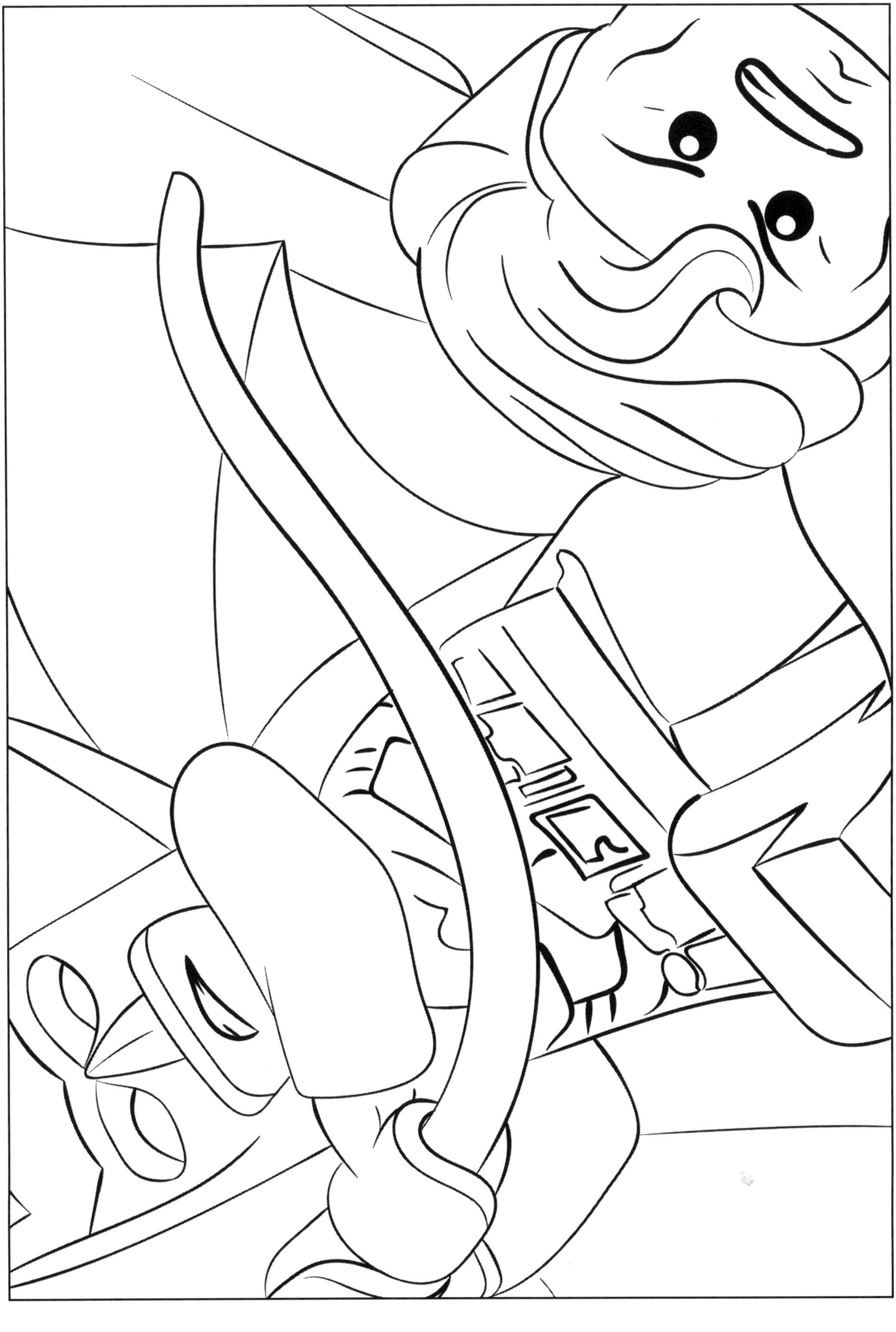

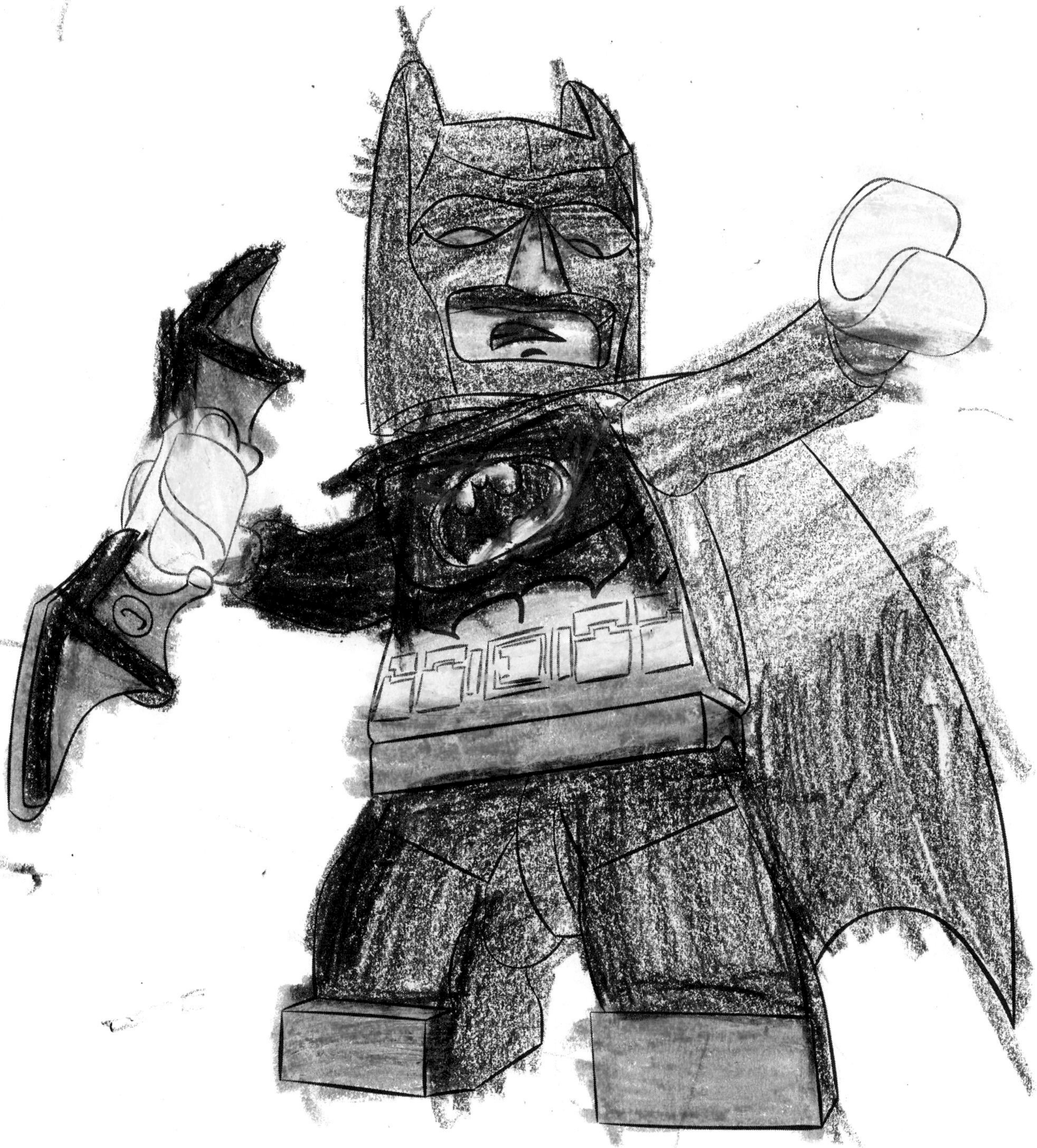

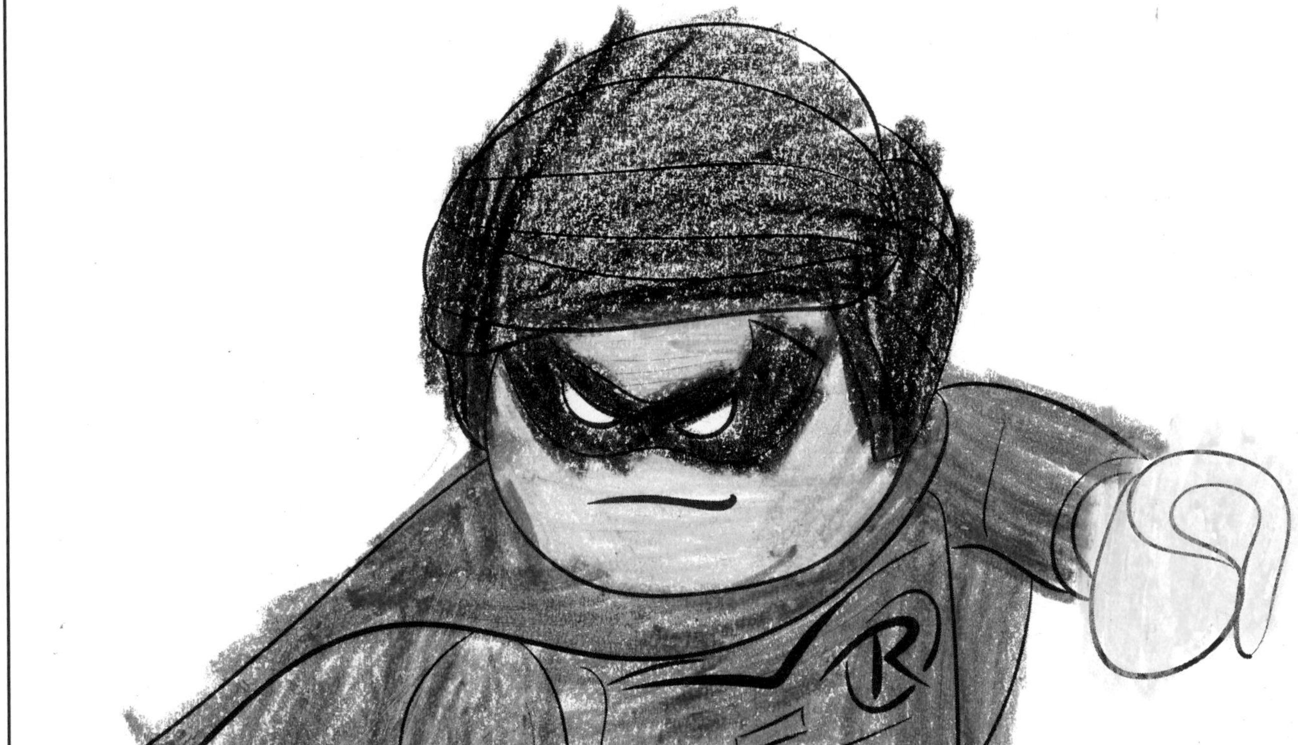

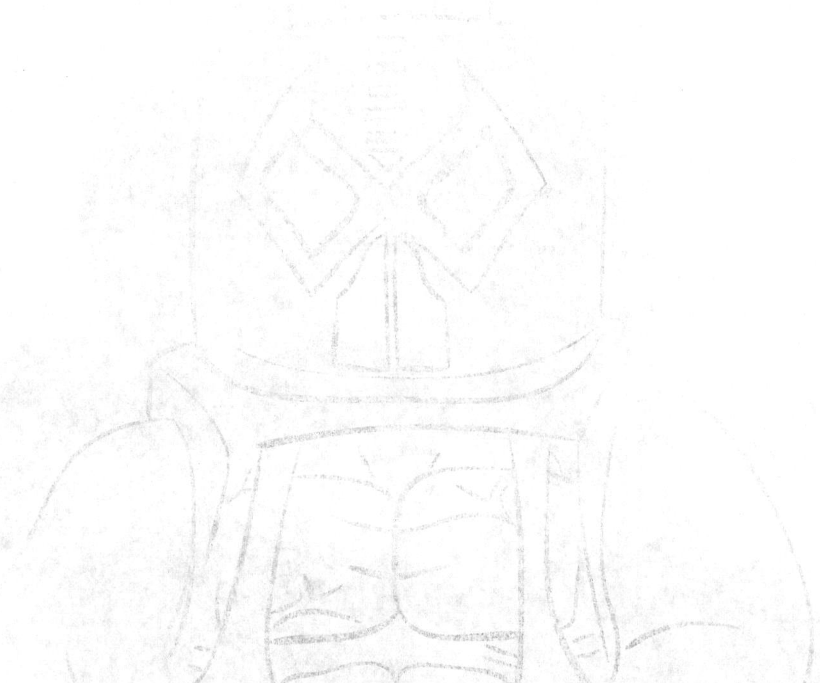

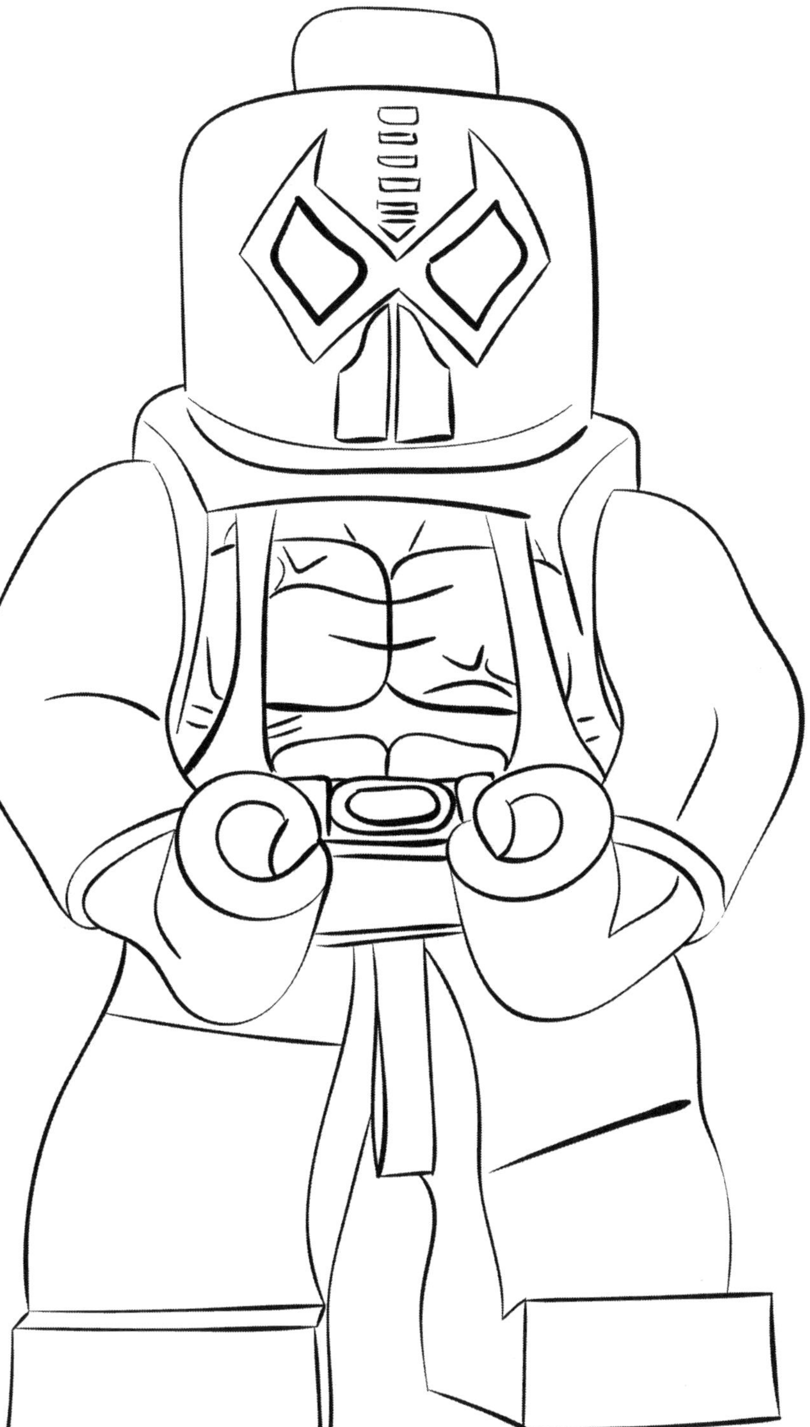

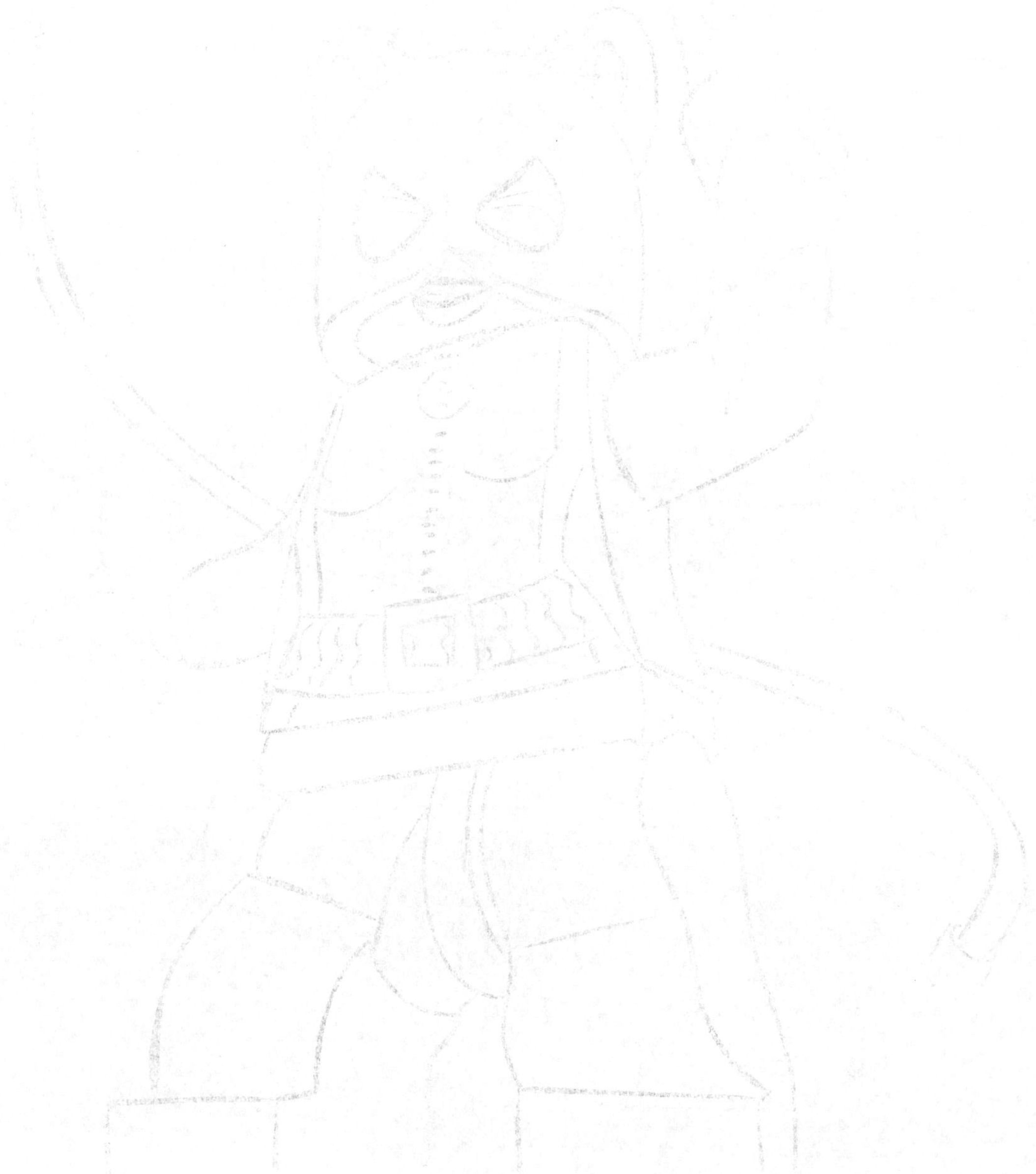

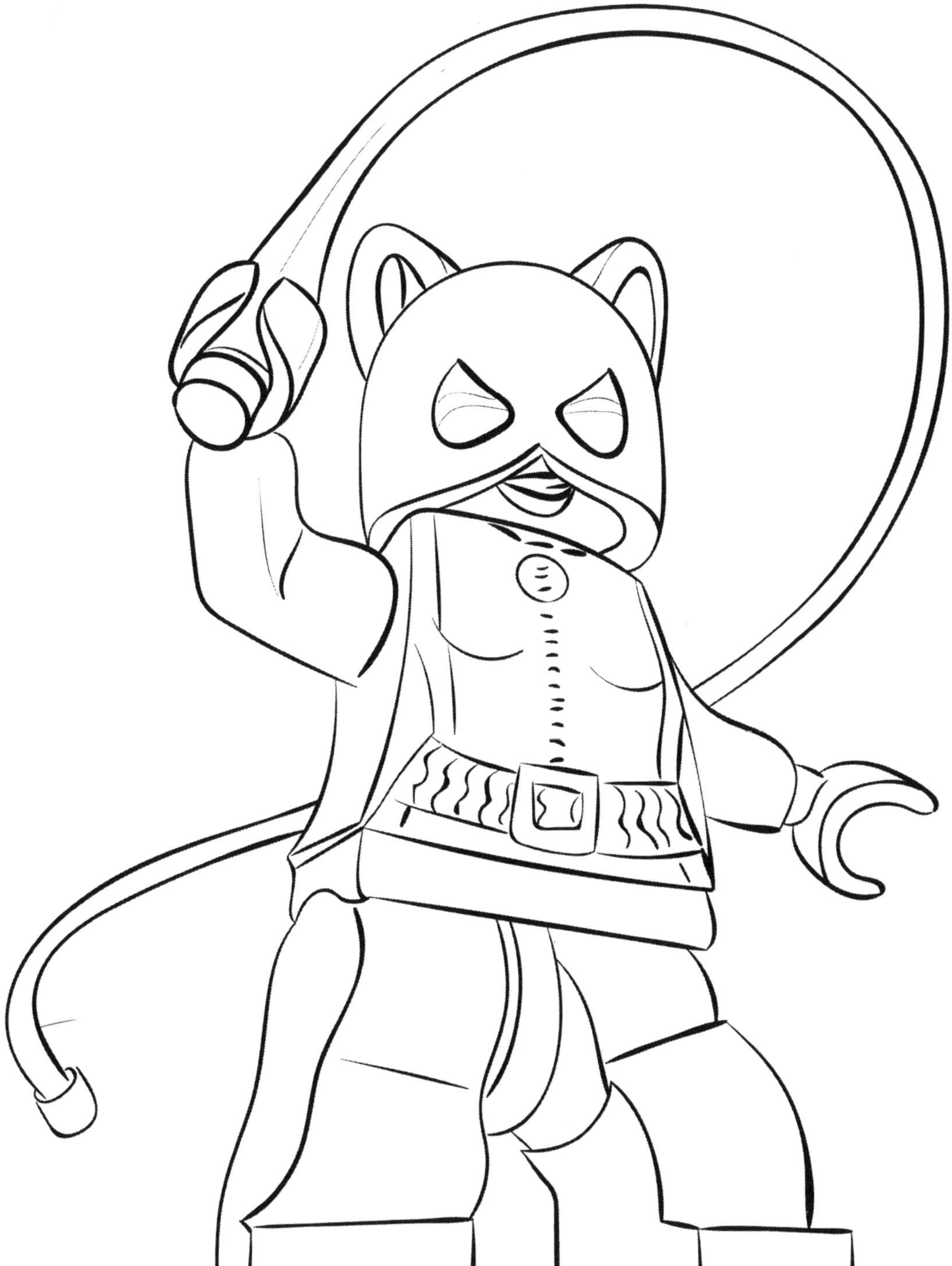

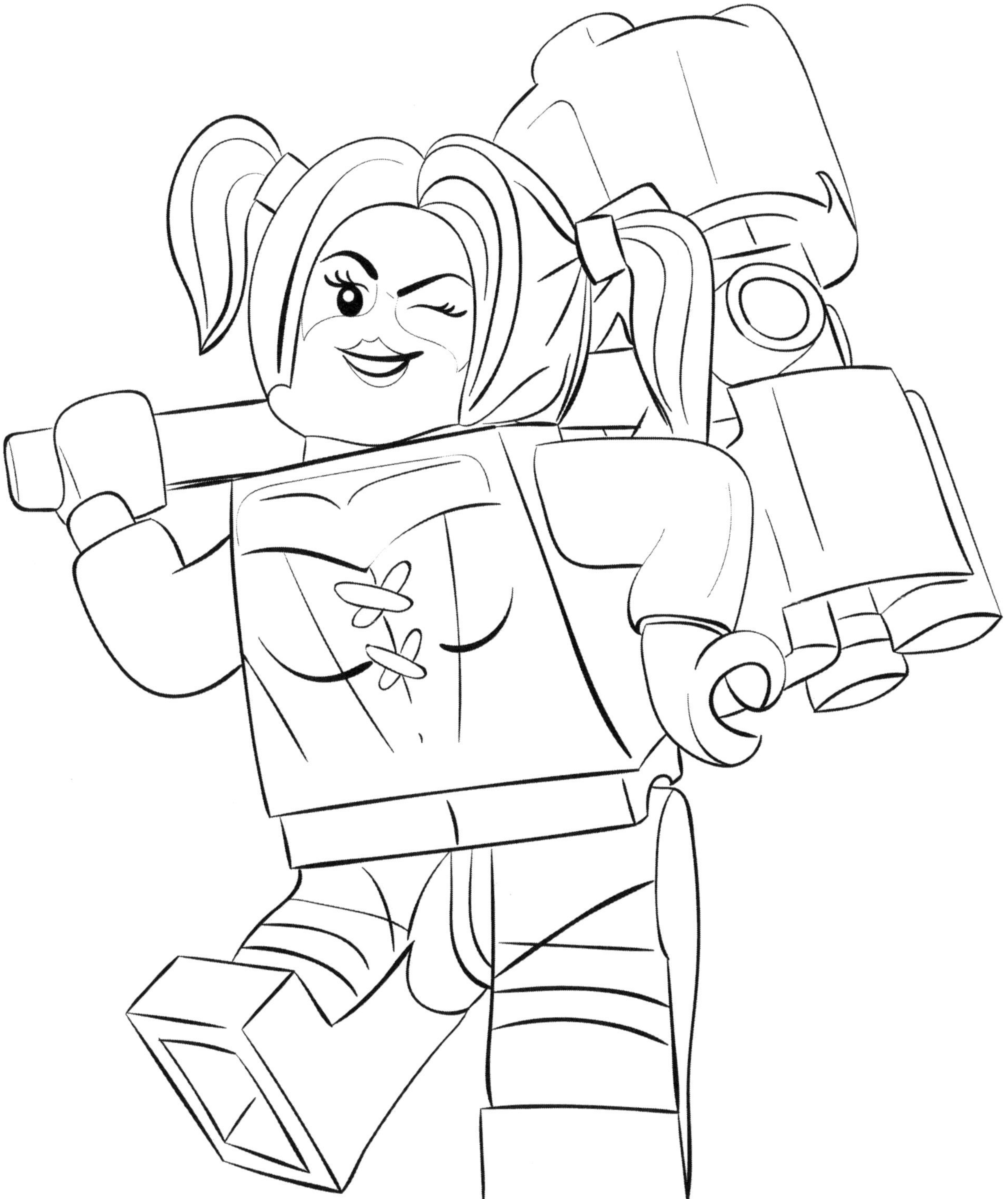

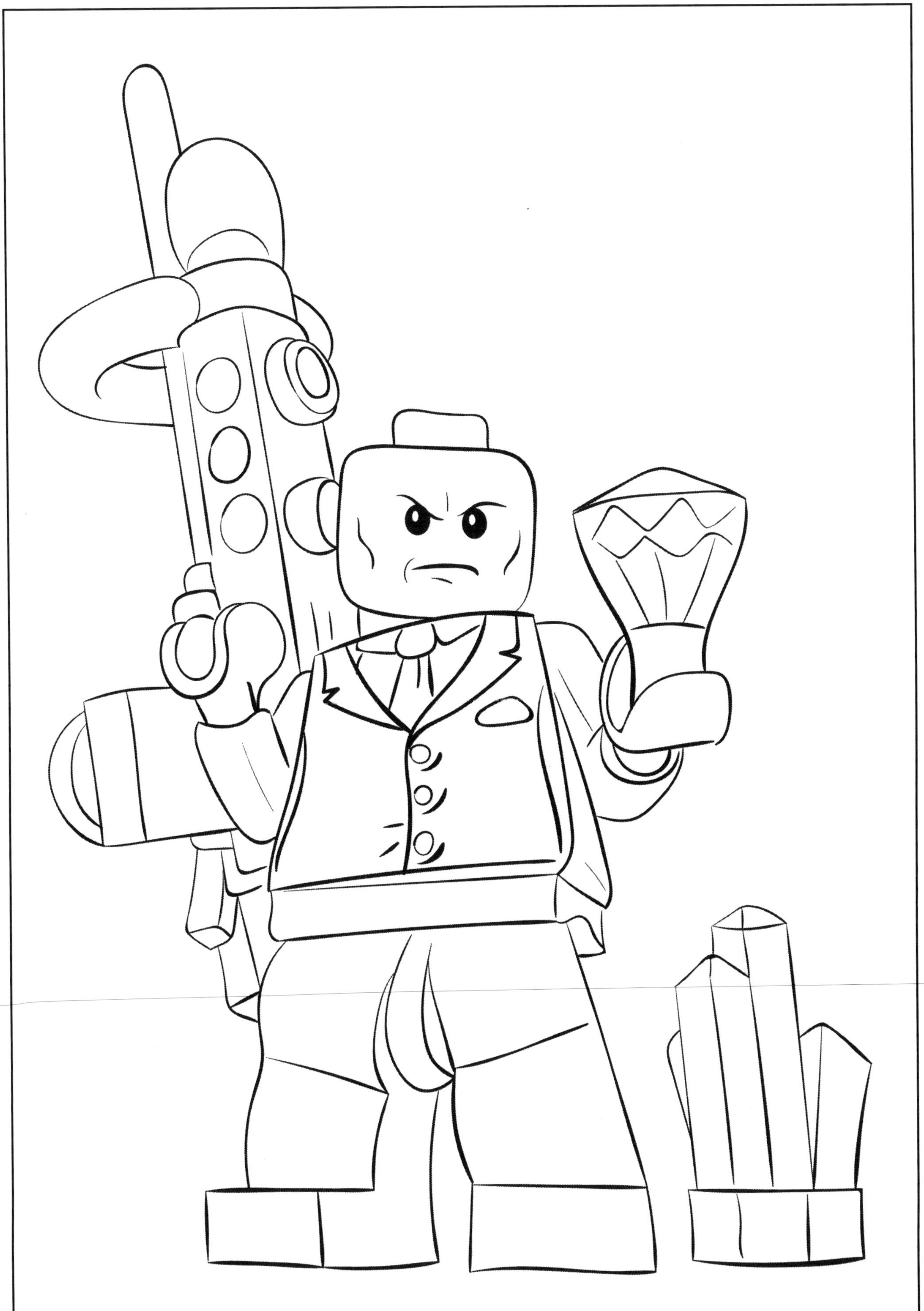

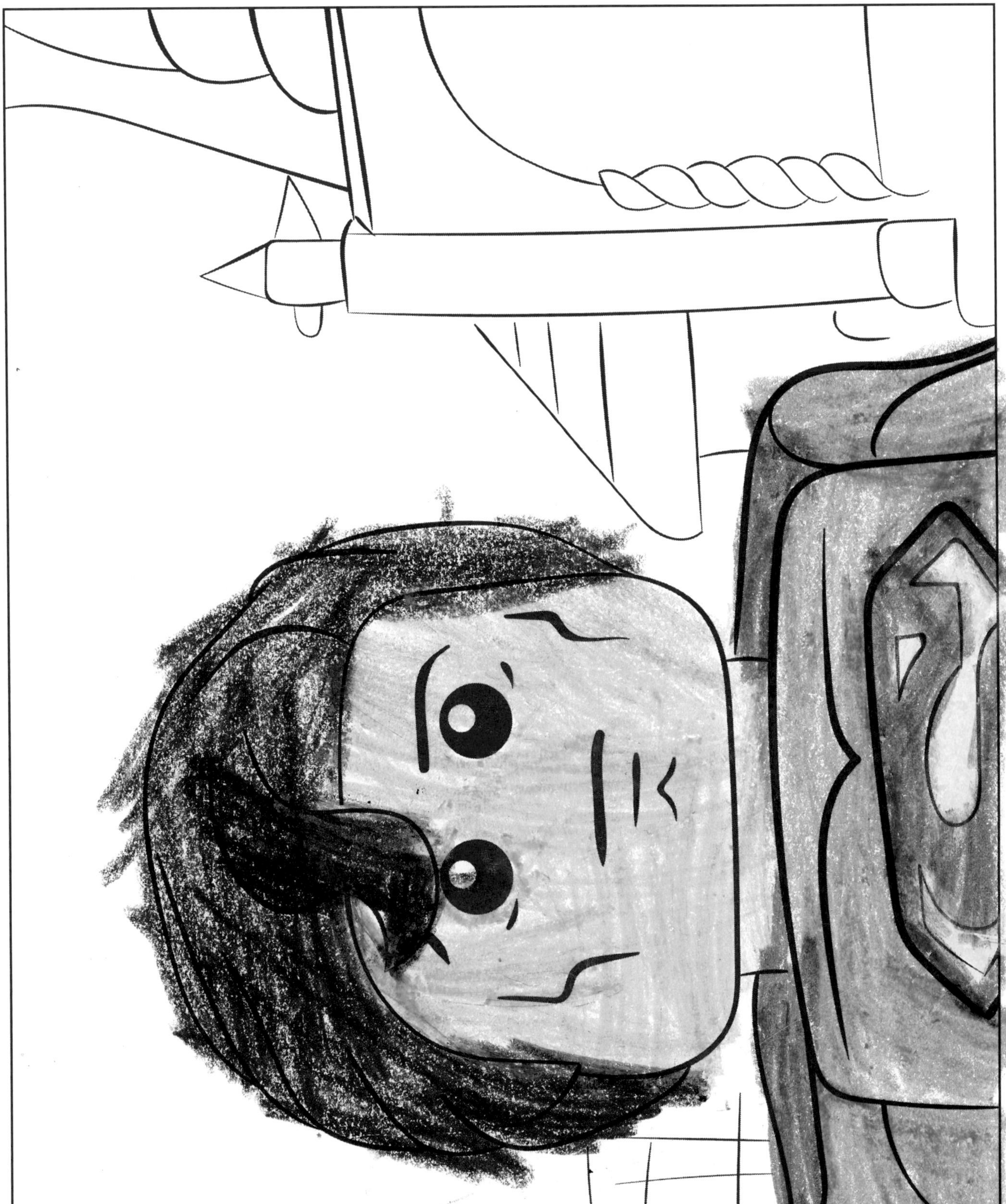

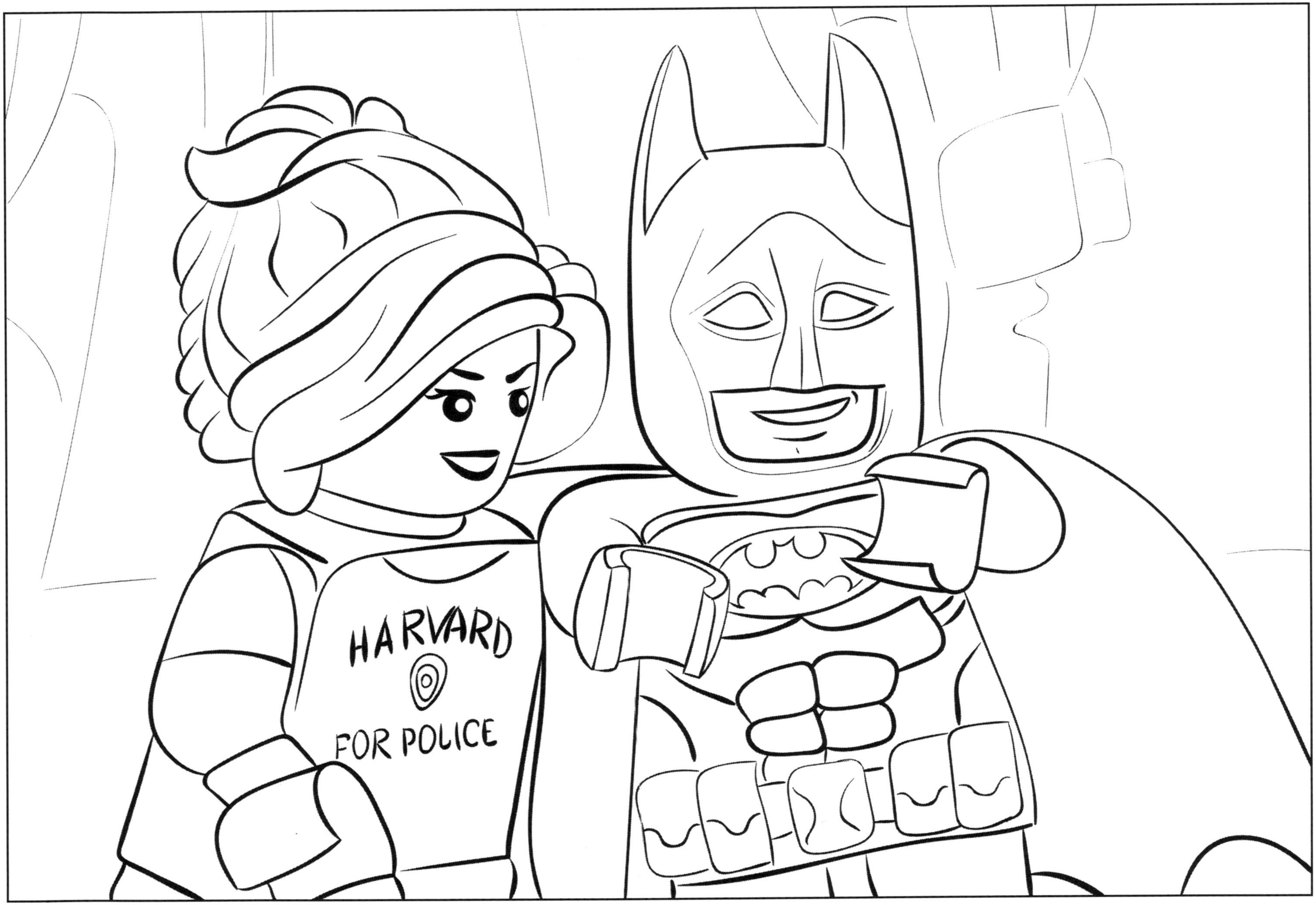
HARVARD
FOR POLICE

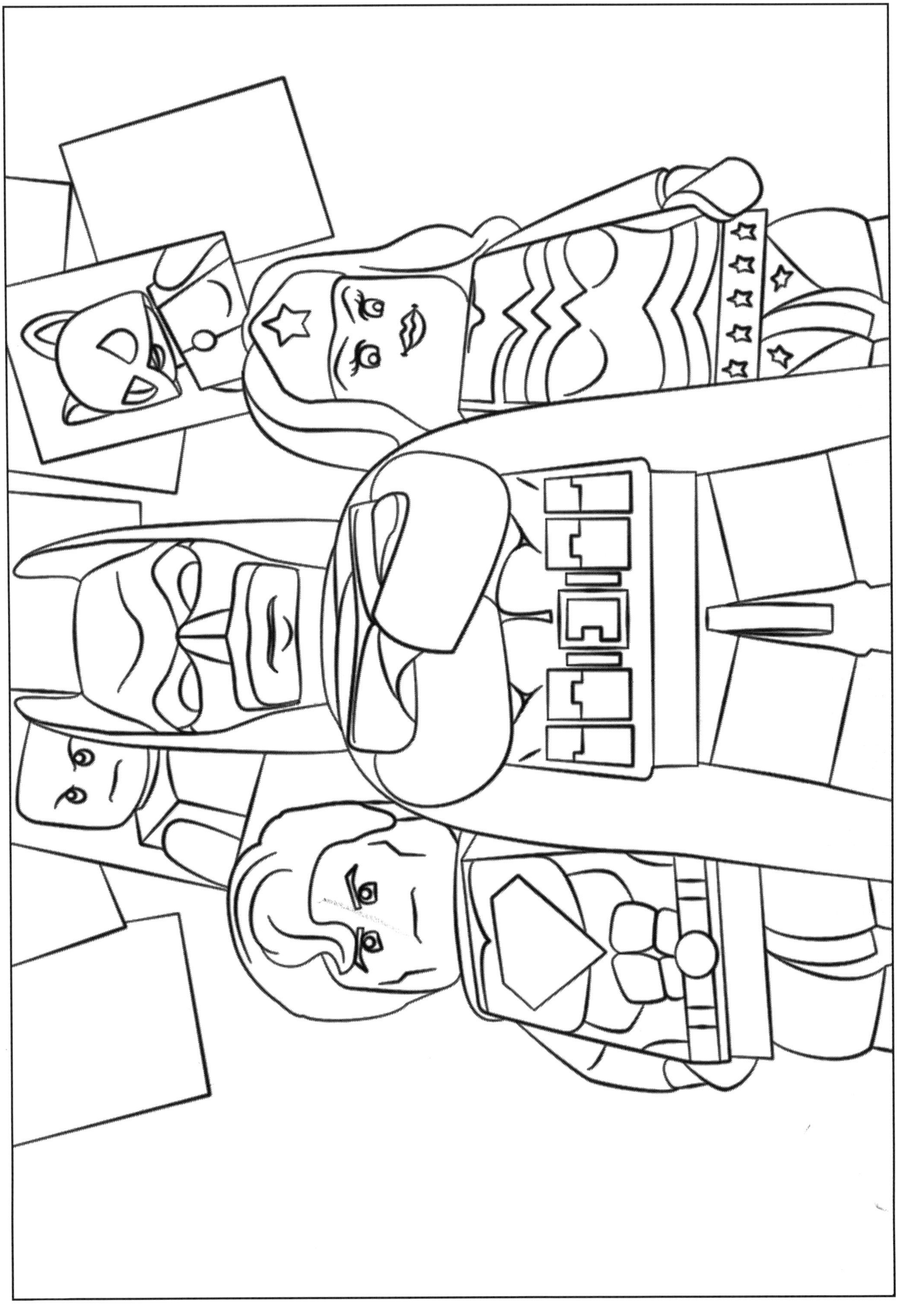

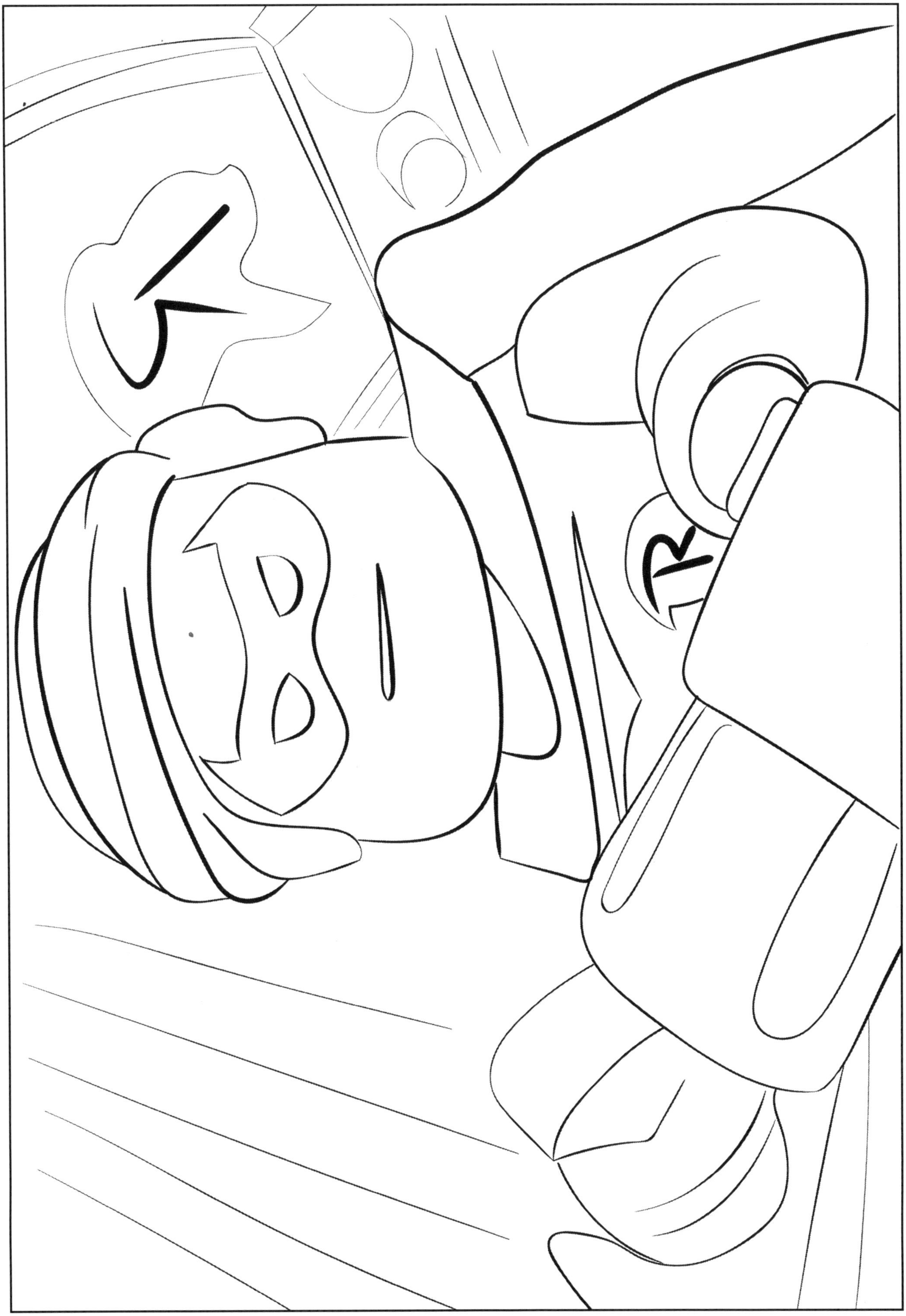

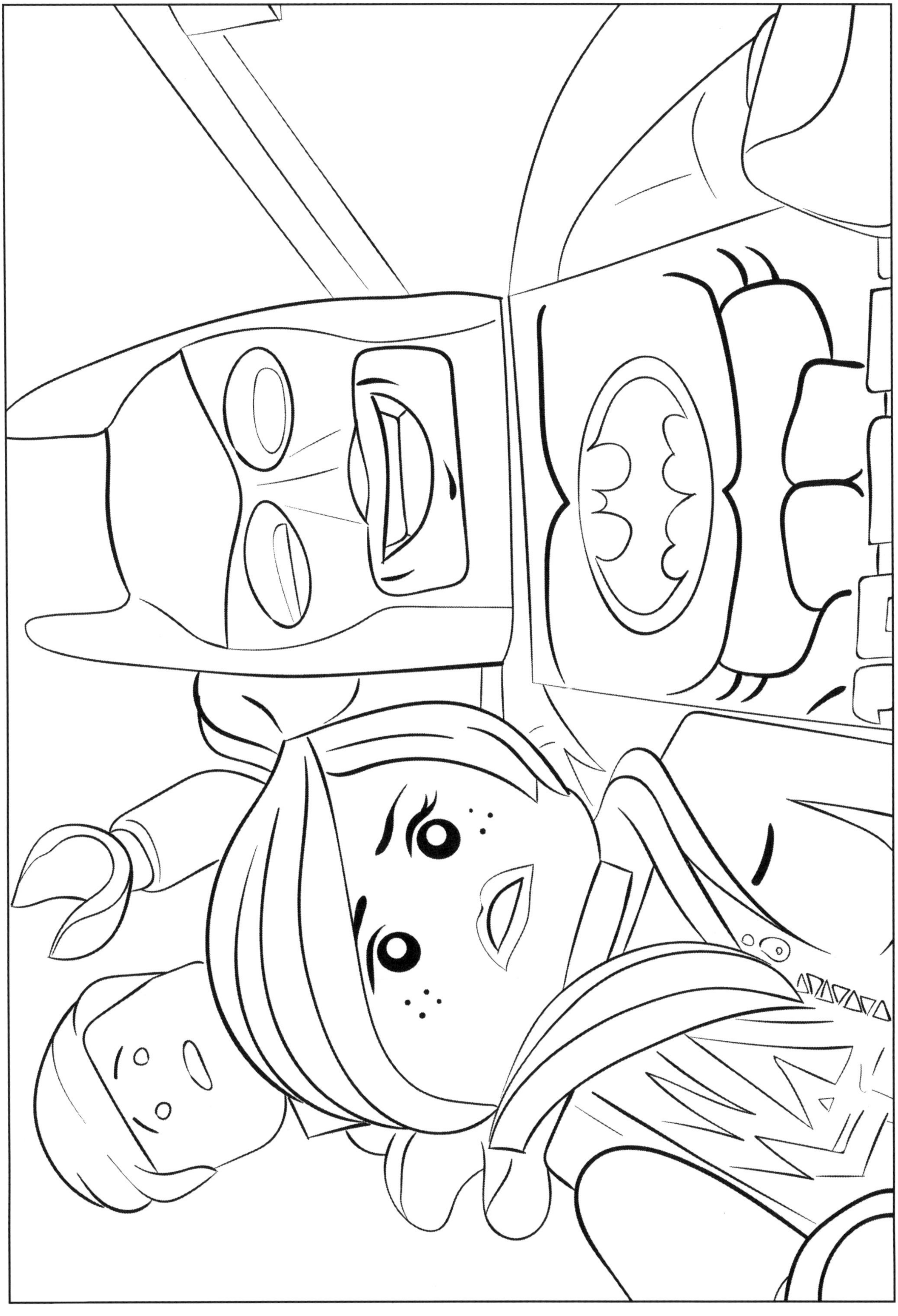

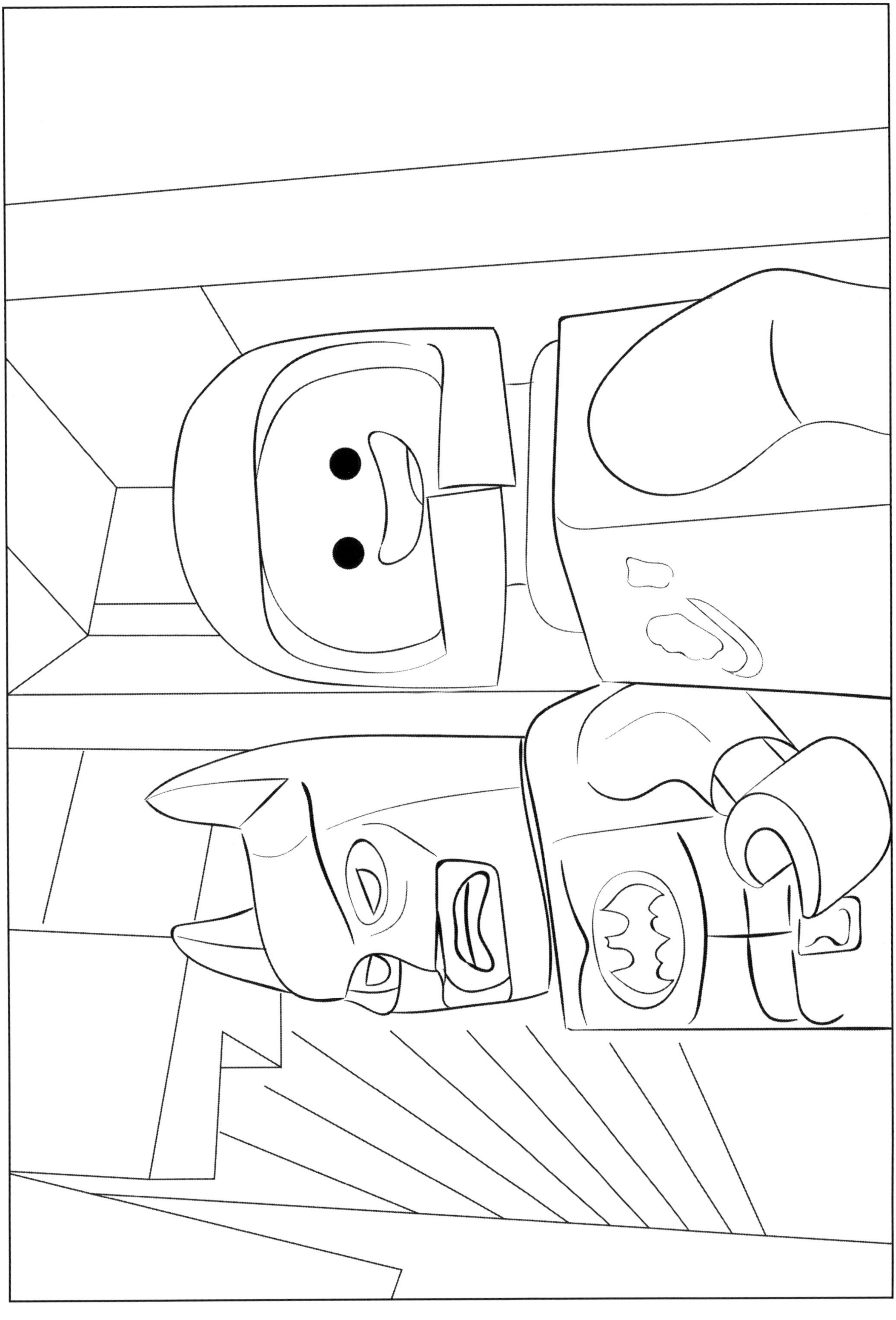

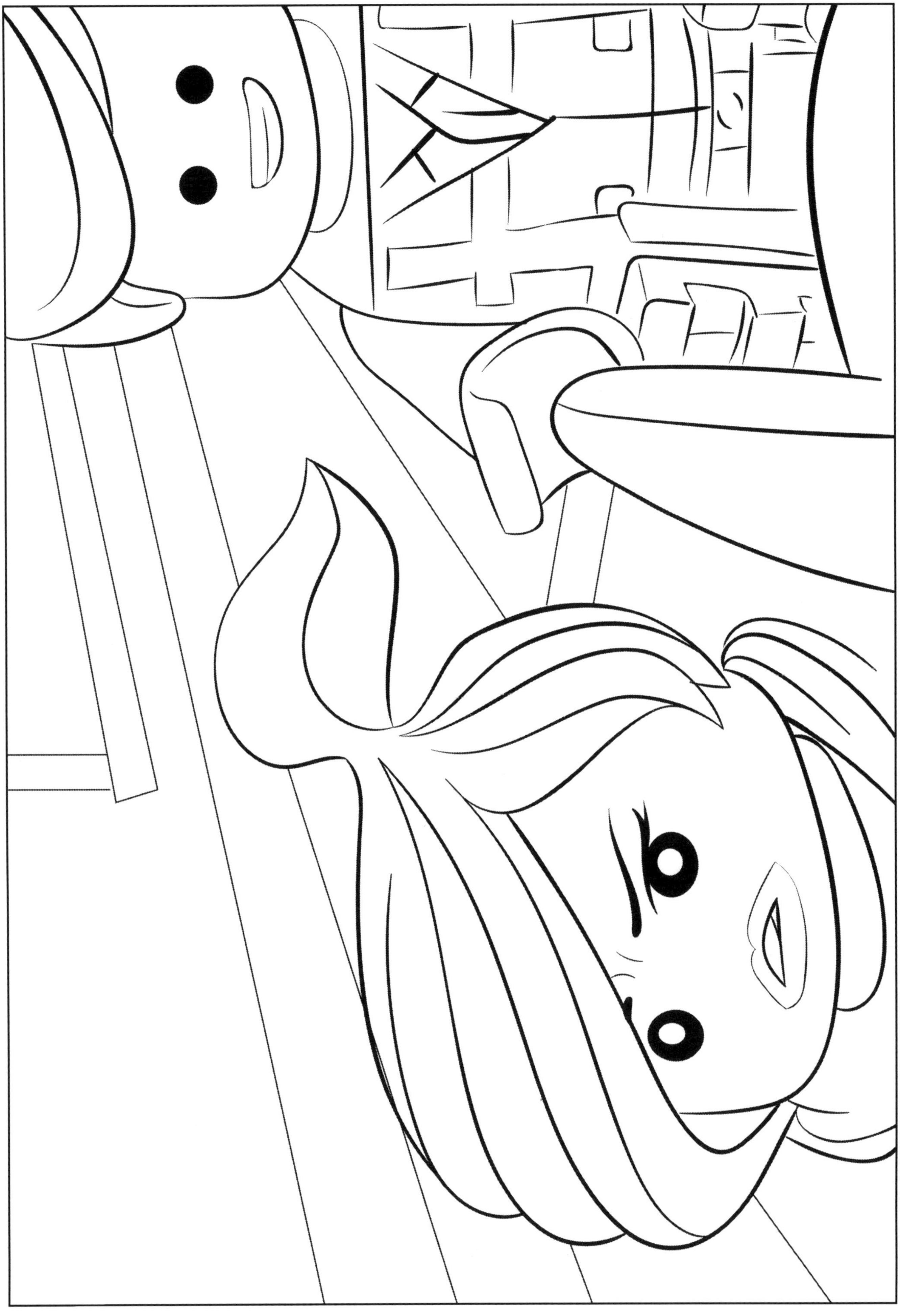

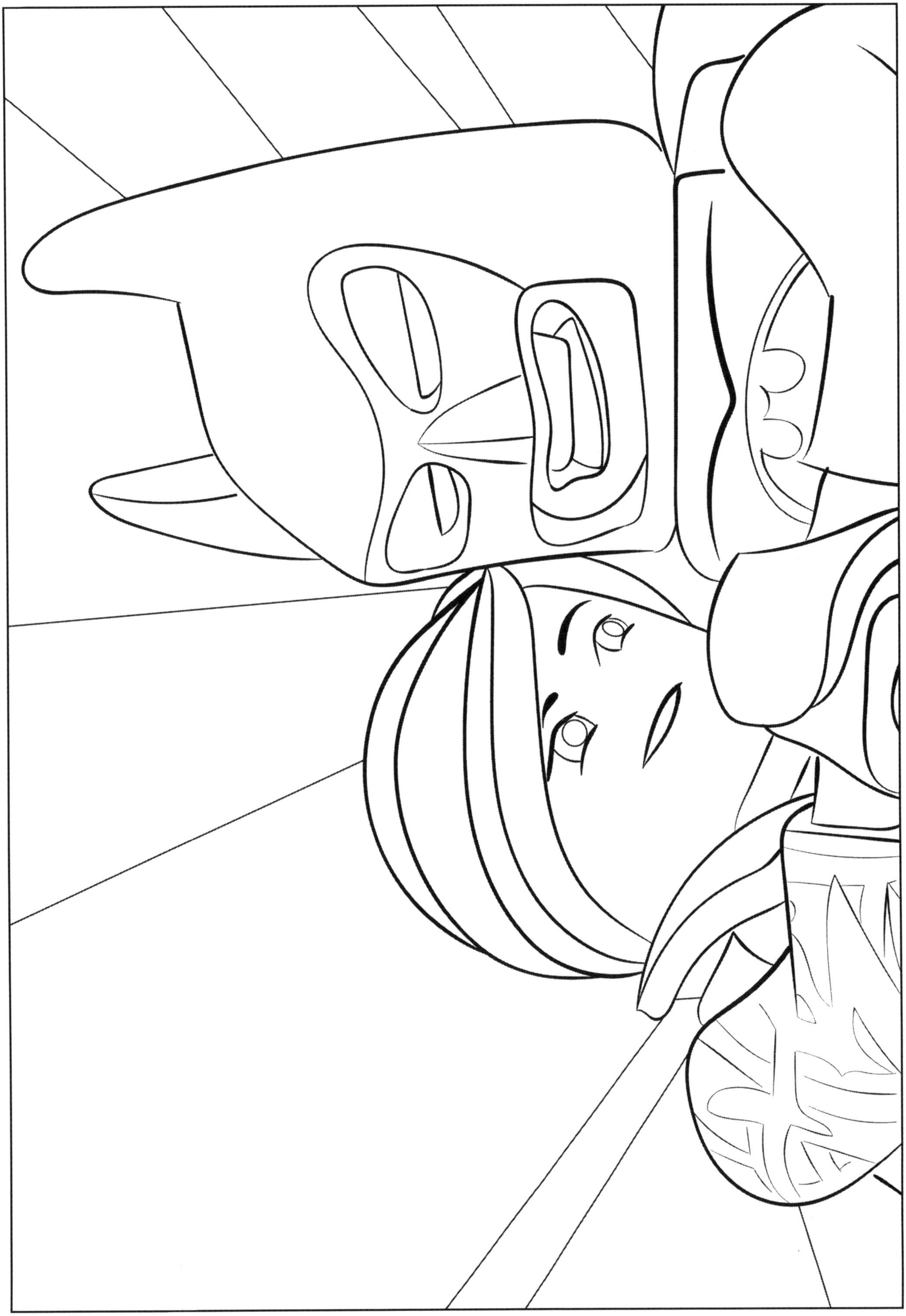

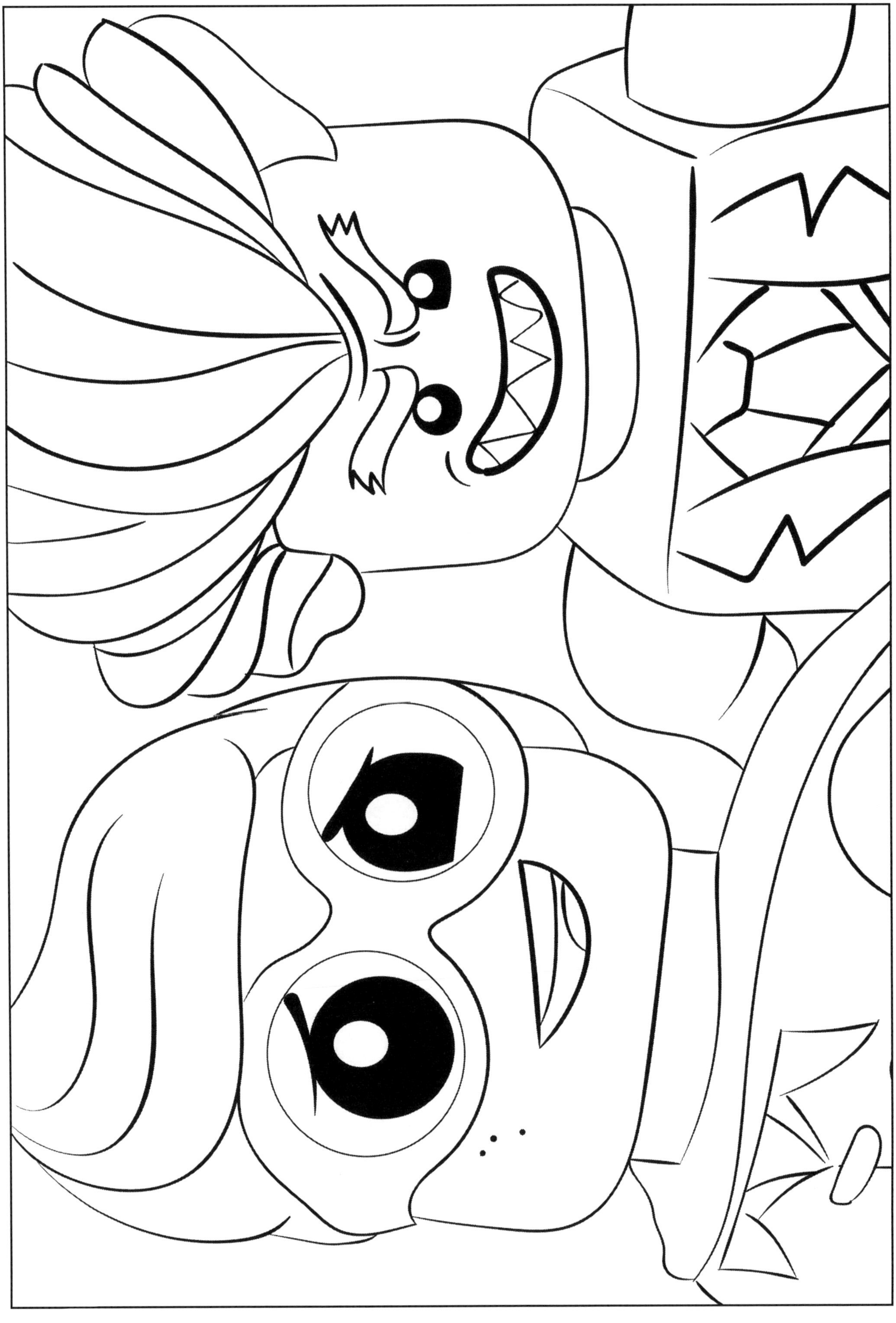

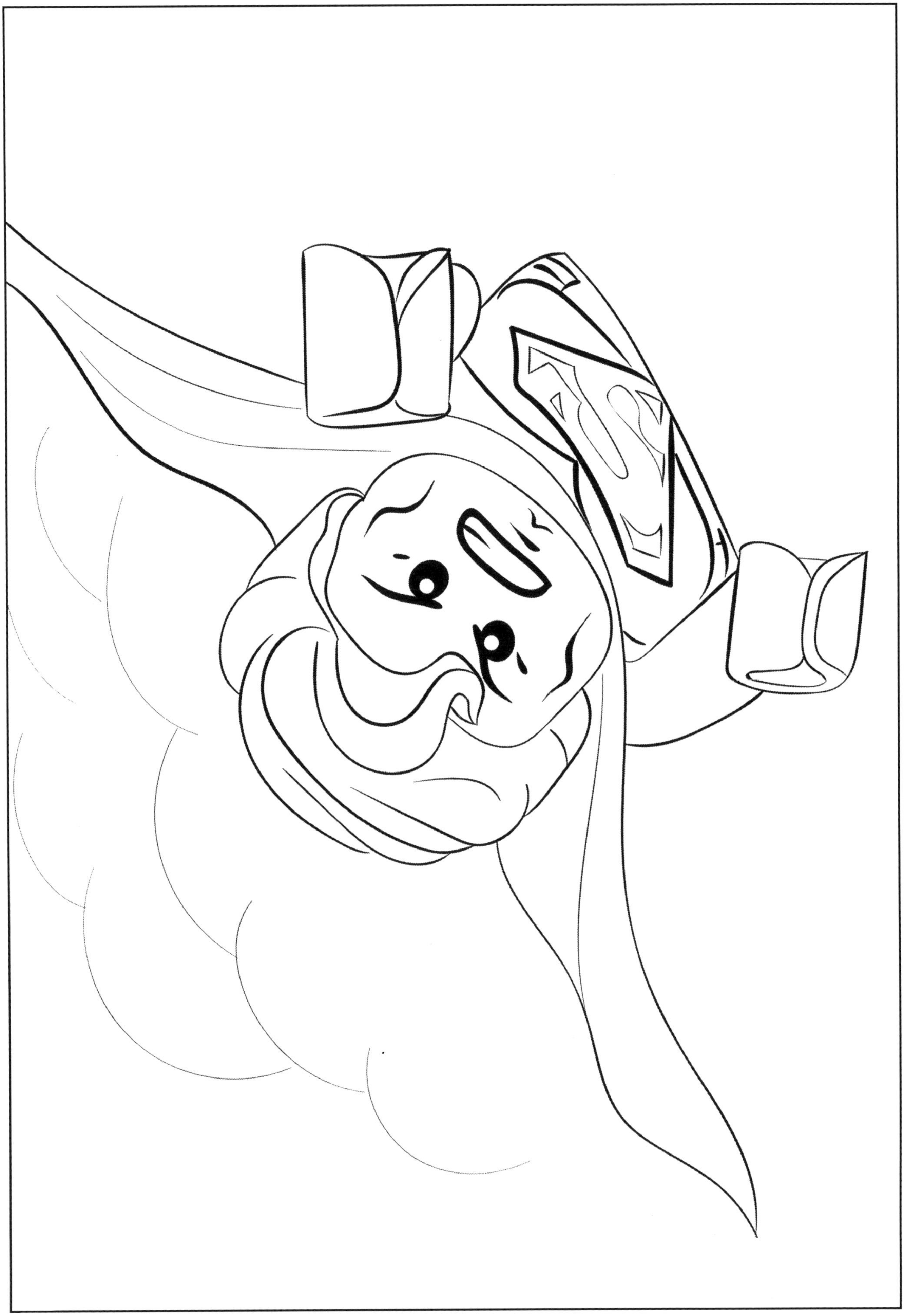

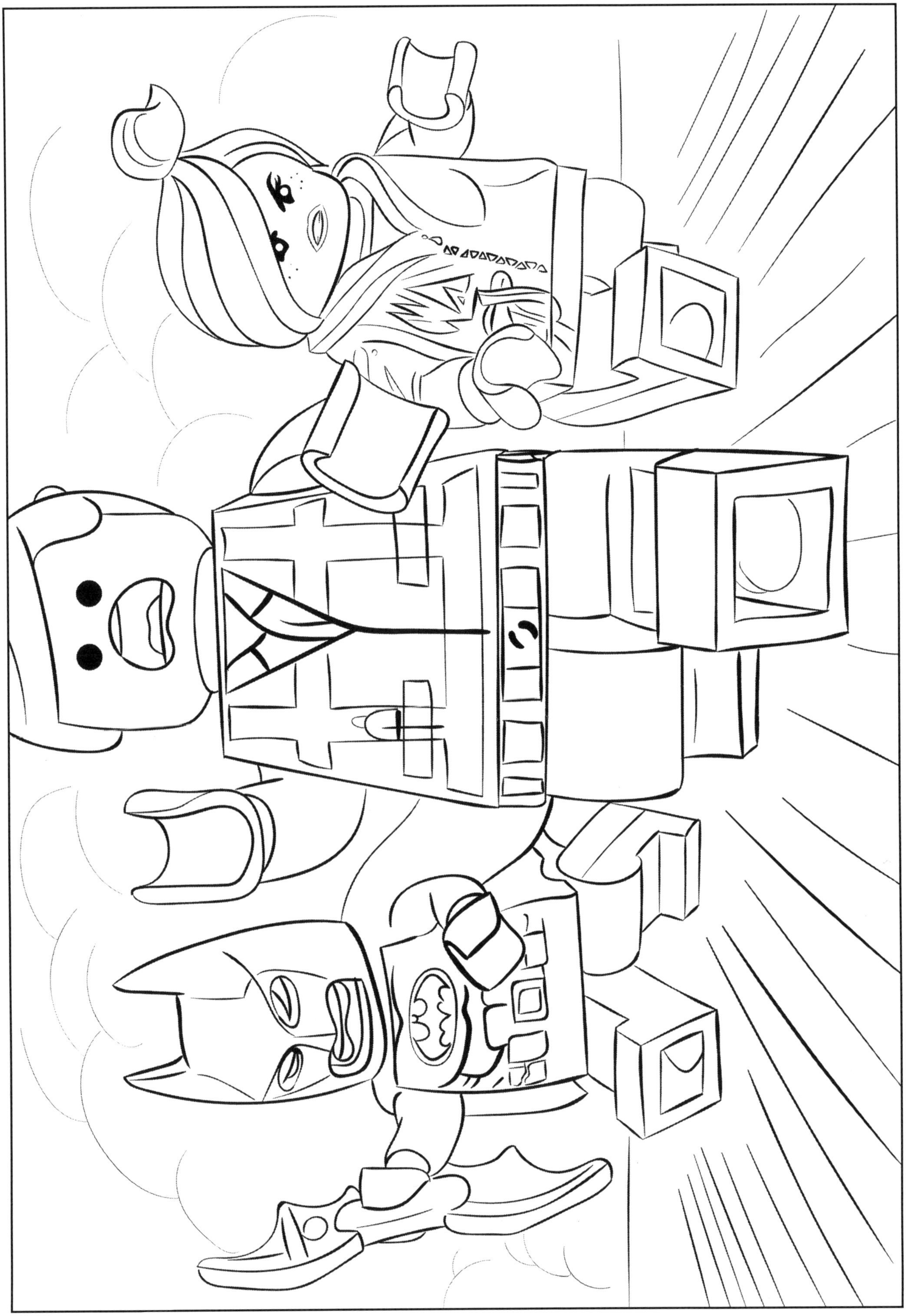

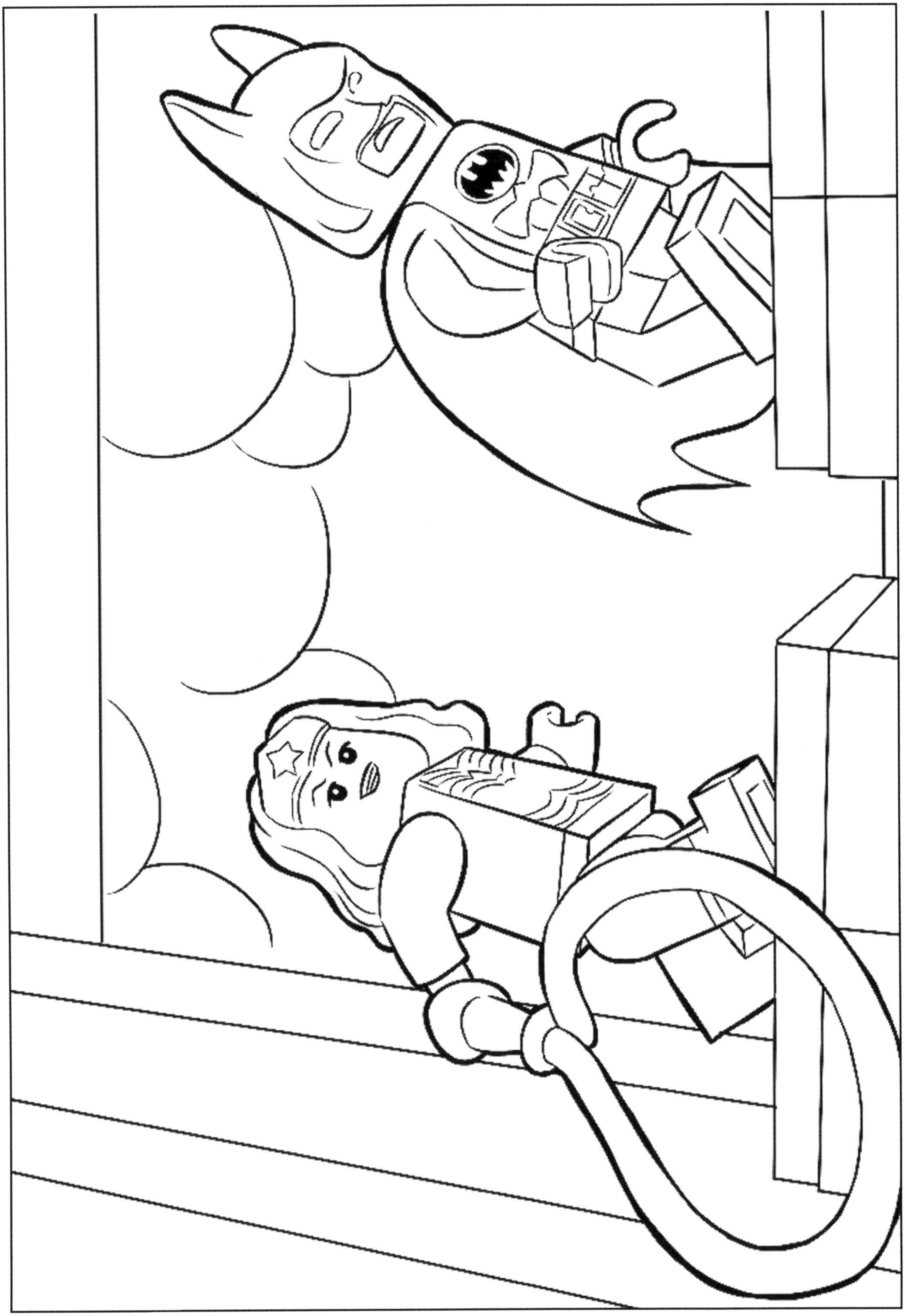

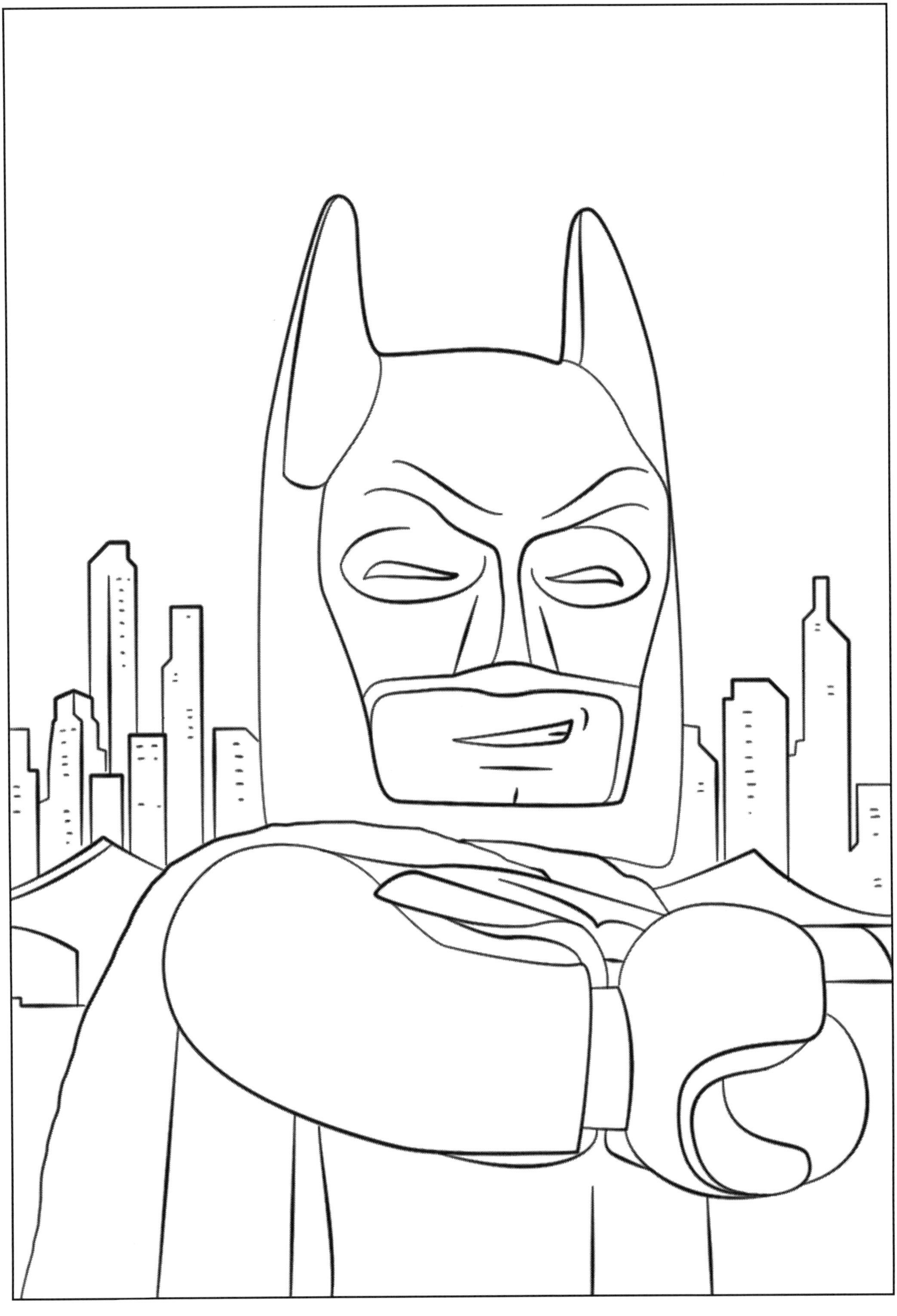

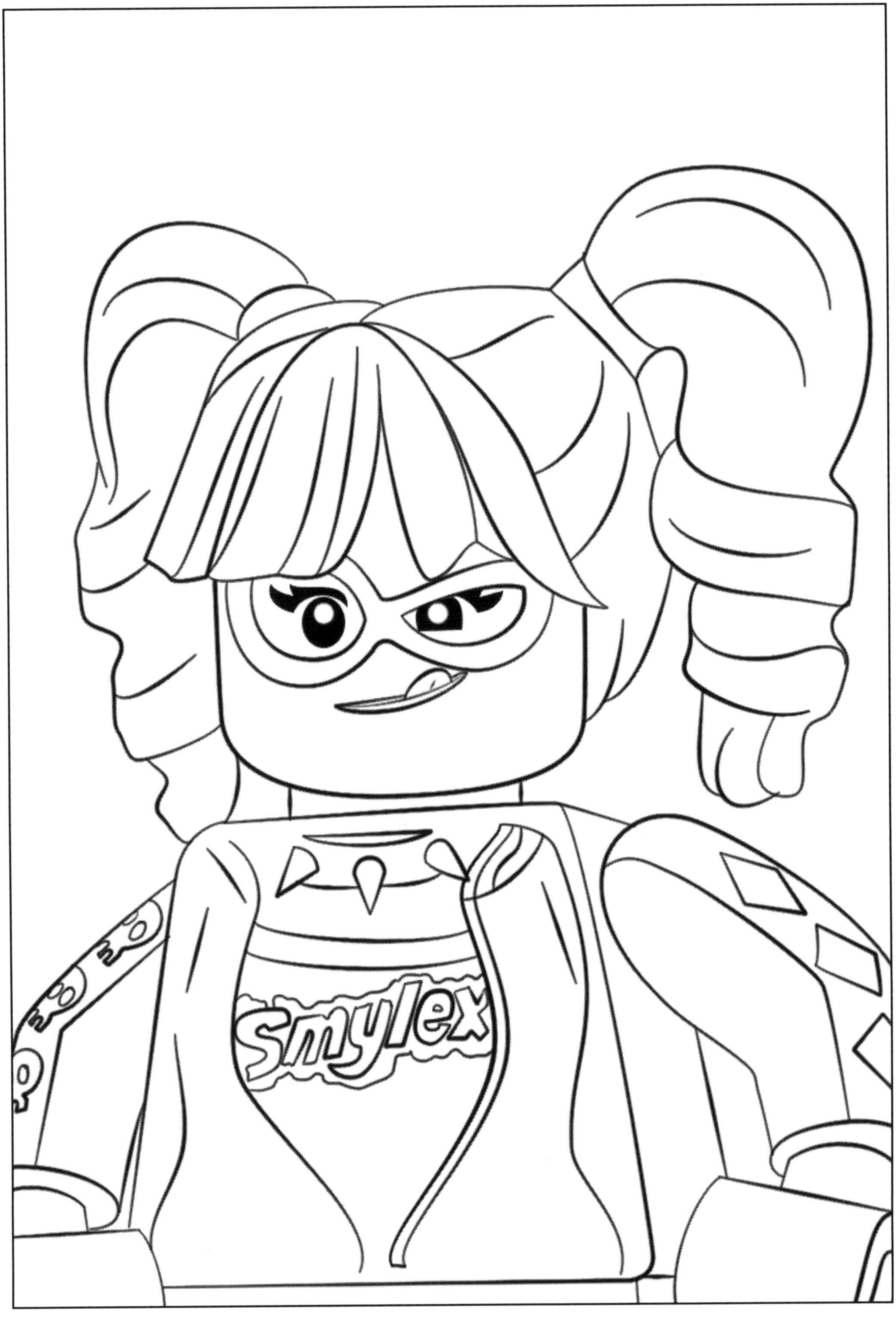
Smylex

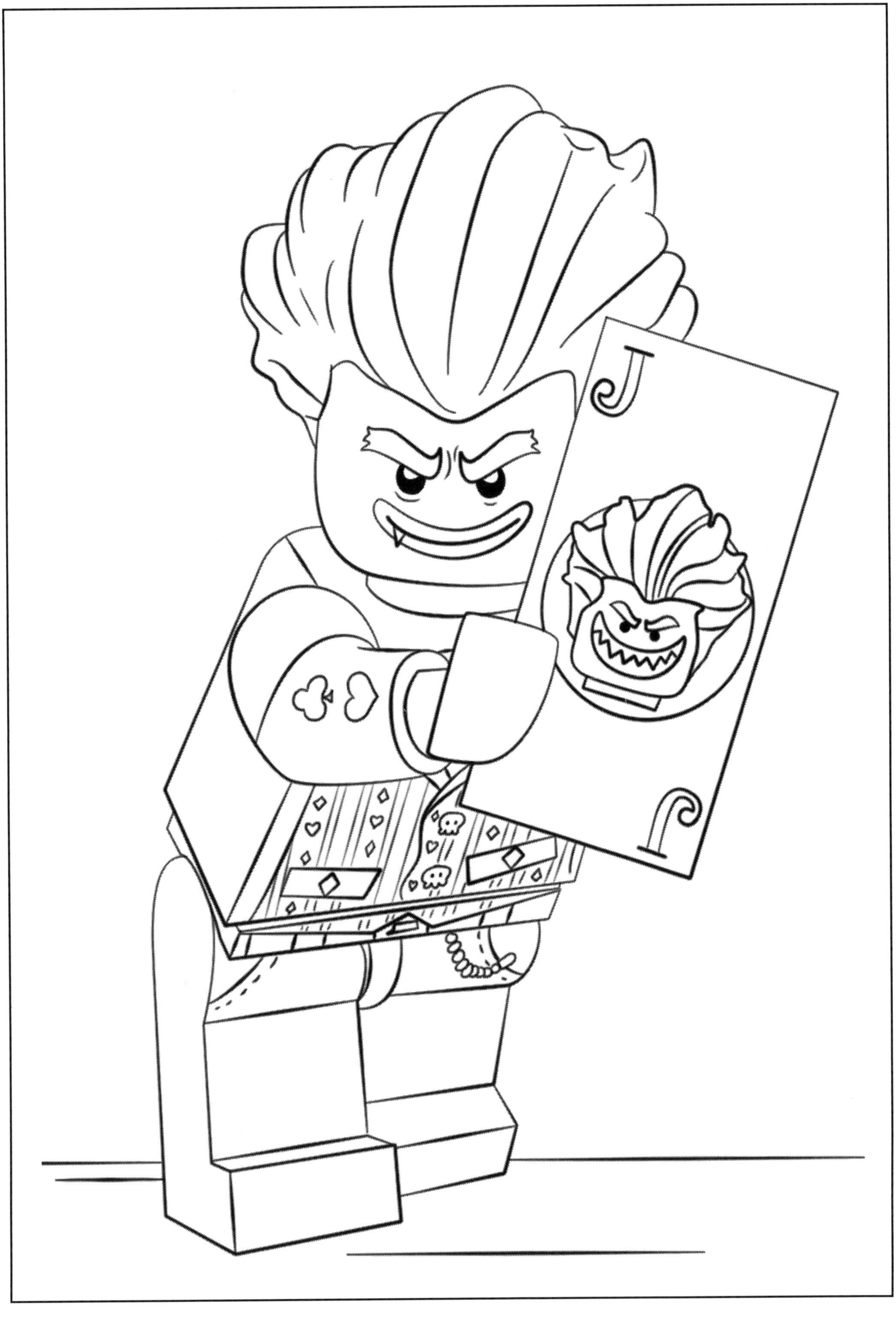
J
J

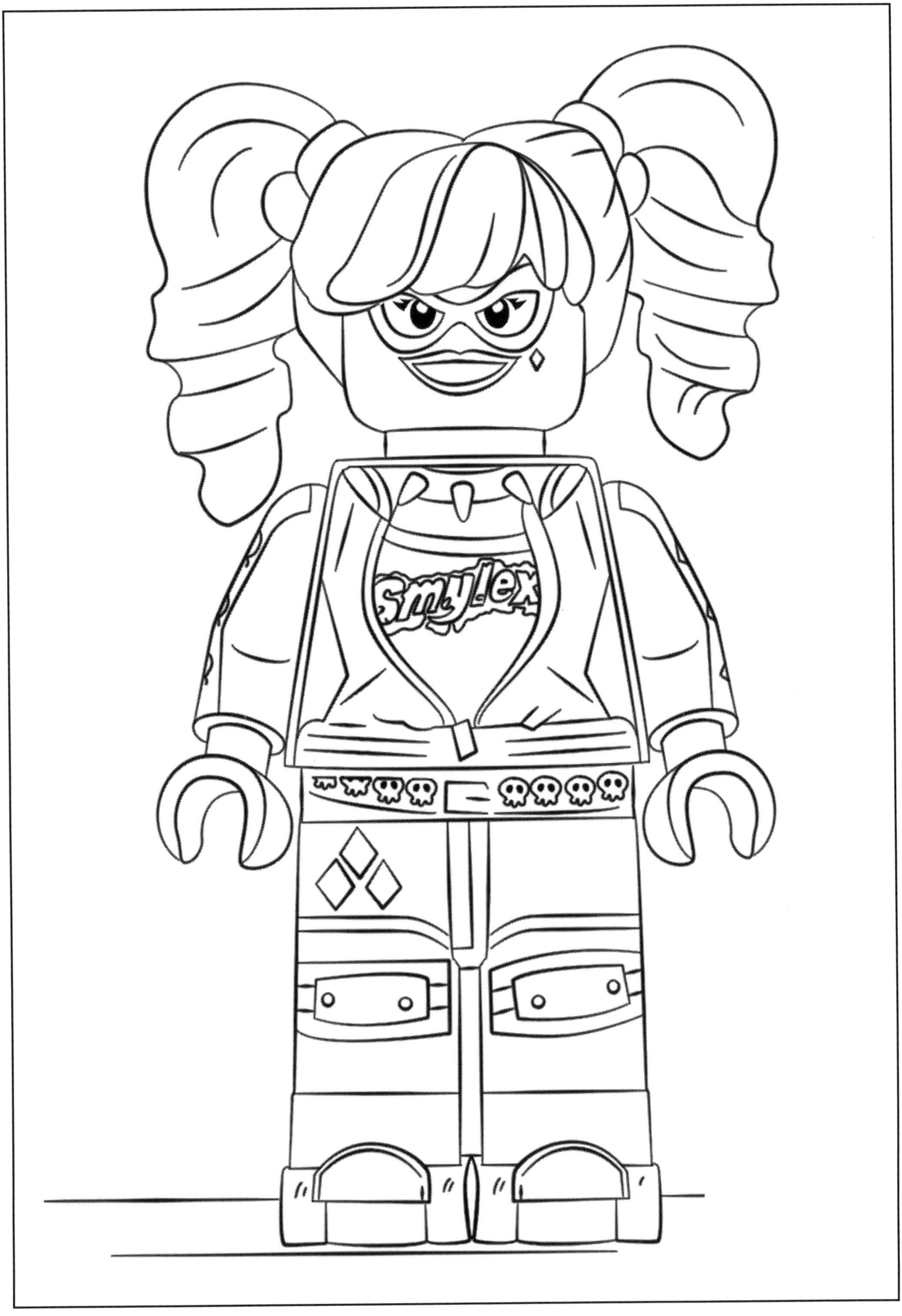
smylex

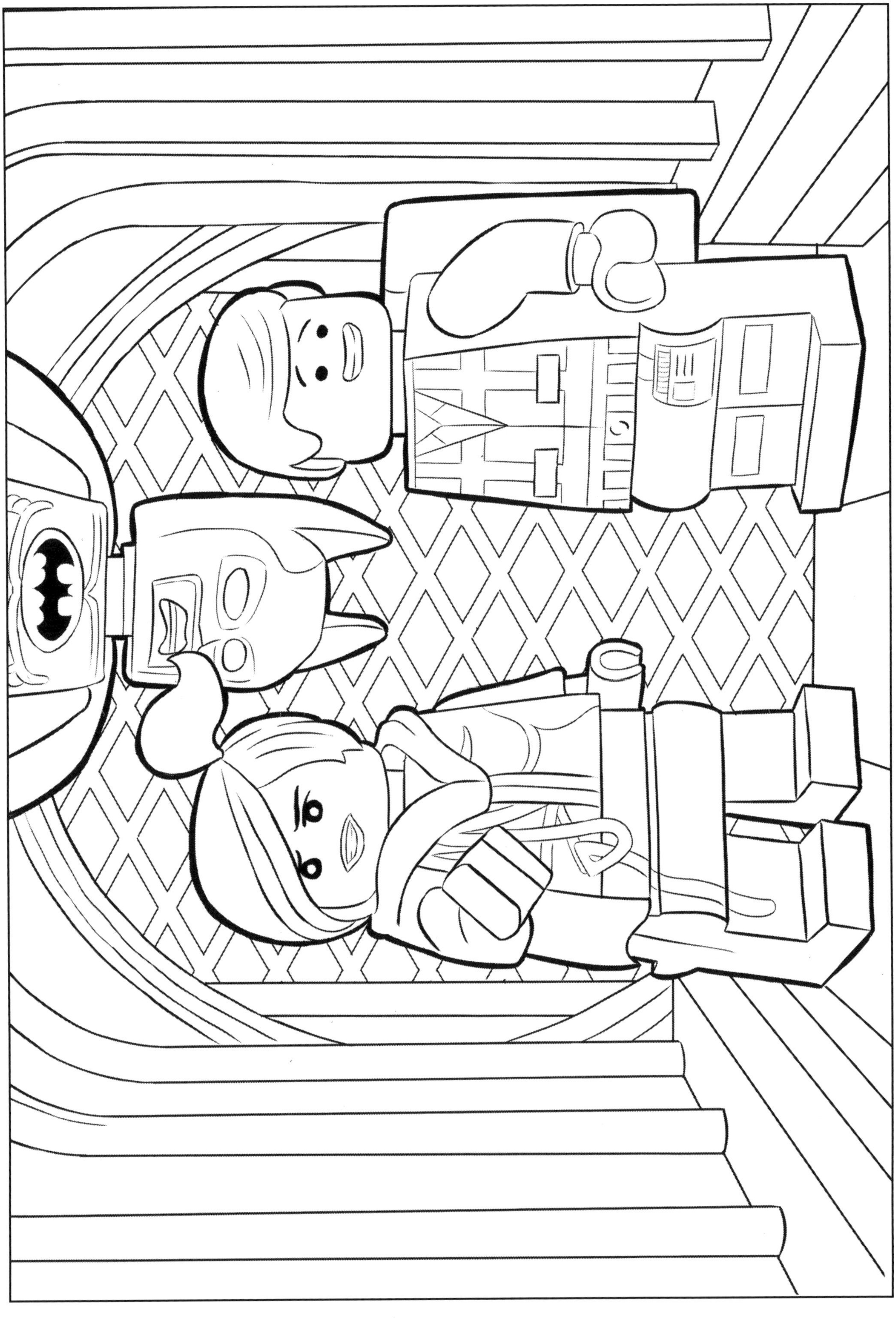

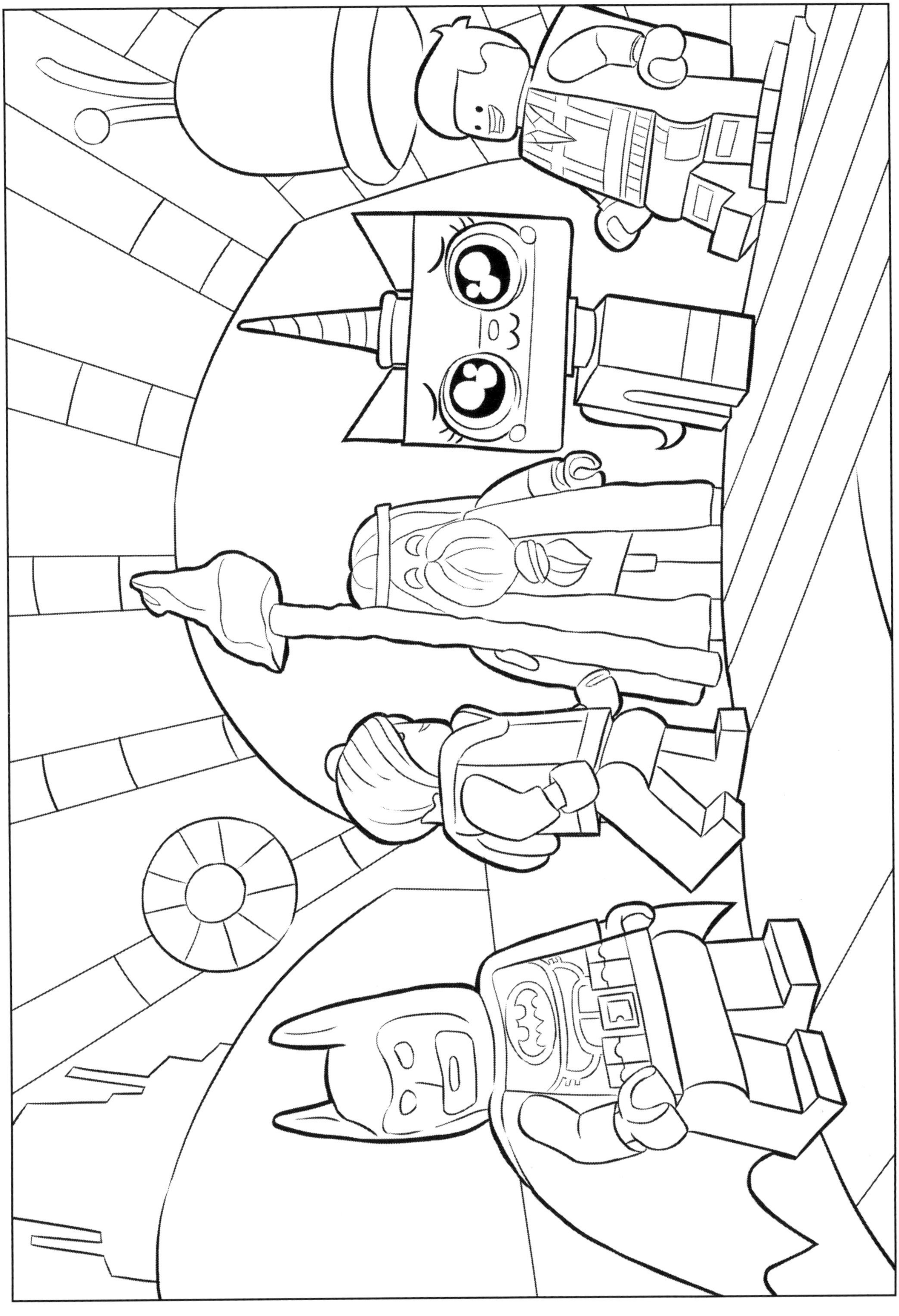

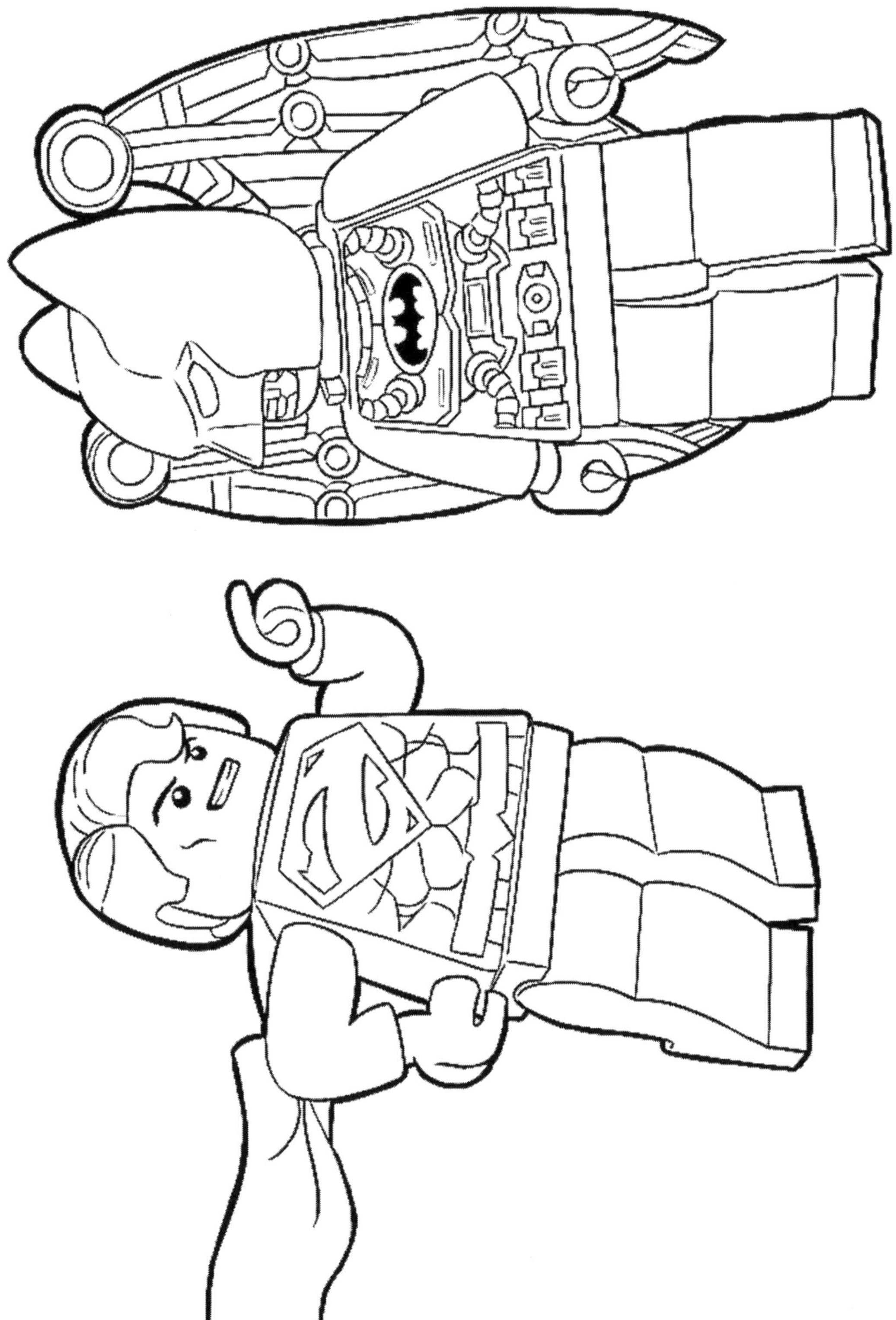

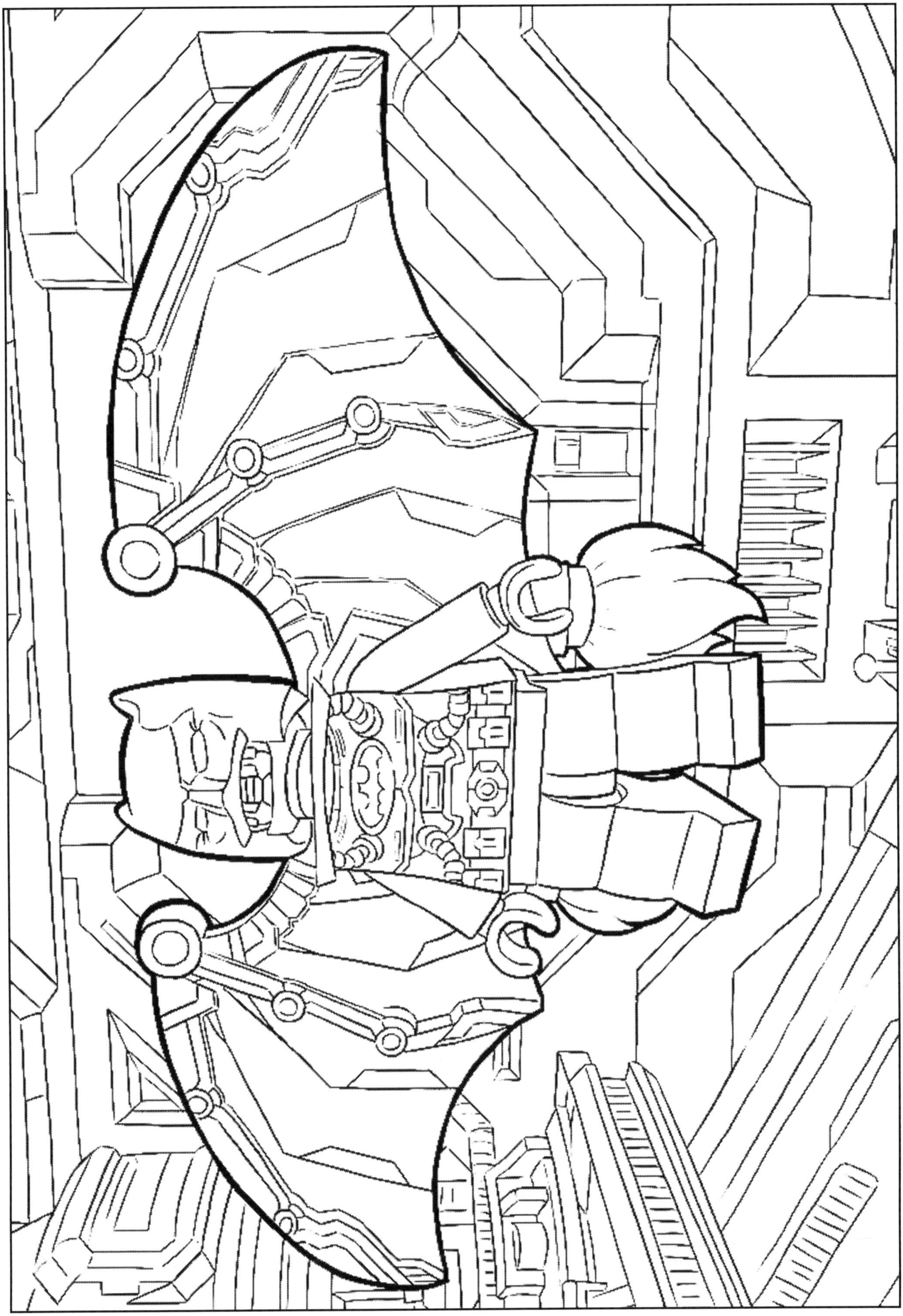

49356659R00035

Made in the USA
Middletown, DE
14 October 2017